G000090164

For Sarah and James

First published by Jacana Media (Pty) Ltd in 2018

10 Orange Street
Sunnyside
Auckland Park 2092
South Africa
+2711 628 3200
www.jacana.co.za

ISBN 978-1-4314-2771-0

Cover design by Mary Duncan
Editing by Russell Martin
Proofreading by Linda Da Nova
Set in MrsEaves 12.5/15pt
Printed by CTP Printers, Cape Town
Job no. 003330

See a complete list of Jacana titles at www.jacana.co.za

VINTAGE
LOVE

AND OTHER ESSAYS

JOLYON NUTTALL

BY THE SAME AUTHOR

*A Literary Friendship: Alan Paton and
Neville Nuttall*

*The First Five Years: The Story of the
Independent Development Trust*

Hooked on Rivers

Contents

Introduction

Early in 2016 I spent two months within a bus ride of the Harvard Book Store in Cambridge, Massachusetts, in the United States. My first visit to the bookshop a day or two after my arrival was in search of a book for a friend in Cape Town. My second visit was to collect it.

It was on that second visit that I wandered down a row of shelves labelled "Essays and Non-Fiction Literature". At the end of the row was a small padded seat tucked into an alcove. For the remaining fifty-five days of my stay, I must have visited the Harvard Book Store about forty more times and almost always it was to that same row and that same little seat in the alcove. There were occasions when the seat was occupied, but as soon as it was vacated, I pounced. From the shelves I withdrew volume after volume of essays by writers who were new to me, with one exception: George Orwell, famed as the author of *Animal Farm* and *1984* but represented here as the essayist on multiple subjects drawn from his own life experiences.

The more I read, the more I became intrigued by the essay as a distinct literary form that I had not recognised as such before. It was neither memoir nor autobiography (Orwell: "Autobiography is only to be trusted when it reveals something disgraceful"). It tended to focus on specific episodes, specific people, specific periods in which the essayist had been involved. It was time-bound. In many of the essays there was a narrative. In these cases, the absolutely crucial factor was that the writer was involved: "I was there – I saw it – I know." In essays of criticism, the writer addressed the issue – whether discussing the works of an author or some contemporary style or cult – in a frank and direct way, without pretence.

When Orwell wrote about poverty, he described his own actual experiences, working as a plongeur (dishwasher) in the fourth basement of a posh Parisian hotel or living as a tramp along with other London down-and-outs on the edge of starvation or joining the British coalminers in their deplorable conditions (*The Road to Wigan Pier*). When he wrote about the Spanish civil war, he was there in the front line, fighting against Franco (and, it transpired, Stalinistas) and took a bullet in his throat.

Among the multitude of other essayists in those shelves in the Harvard Book Store, he became my model in terms of any writing I proposed to do.

And so it has happened. I have written a series of essays drawn from direct experiences in my own life. Everything I have included in this collection of late life writings happened to me. In the Orwellian sense, I was there. I have found that the focus this has brought to my writings has been astonishing. Abandoned has been any sequential connection between the essays as might have happened had I been writing an autobiography. All the items are constructed from episodes in my life that stand out in my memory as significant.

They have not been written in any chronological order. The first essay in the collection, "Can You Cook?", deals with an incident that occurred in the later stages of my life yet it was indeed the first one I wrote. The last piece, "Living Alone", was not the final essay. Its theme came to me while I was in the middle of compiling this collection and it seemed important that I write it there and then. Other essays emerged as I became ever more comfortable in harnessing the medium as the literary form in which I wanted to express myself. The events in "Greyton Passeggiata" happened before my eyes one late Friday afternoon as I was sitting on the stoep of a hostelry in that Cape village, and I wrote it the same evening. "A Summer in New York" required a much deeper dip into memory as did my stories on life as a child and on some of the agonies and delights of growing up.

I have tried at all times to say something interesting and something fresh, in particular on subjects that have been written about extensively by others. For example, to be justified, the essay entitled "The Alan Paton I Knew" needed to bring to light aspects of Paton's life and character that had not been featured previously. I am indebted to my good friend Rod Lloyd for drawing this to my attention after he had read the first draft of the essay. In "On Being a Grandfather", I avoided any sentimental descriptions of dangling dear little creatures on my knee while they gurgled sweet nothings at me. Instead, I have written about how much I have learned from them, how direct and devastatingly frank they are, how deeply they feel and how fully they enjoy.

My readings from those richly endowed Harvard shelves brought home to me what a long tradition of essay writing Orwell inherited, dating back to the sixteenth century and reaching something of a peak in the eighteenth century when Samuel Johnson, William Hazlitt and

Charles Lamb ("A Dissertation upon Roast Pig") perfected the form. When I returned to Cape Town from my sojourn at Harvard, I found on my own shelves three separate volumes of *English Critical Essays*, dating from the sixteenth to the nineteenth century, which I had studied in English II at university and which were last opened in 1953. I also rediscovered the ultimate example of the titling of such essays from the twentieth-century volume by Hilaire Belloc, which he called *On* and in which twenty-four of the thirty essays in the collection began with that single word, ranging from "On Mumbo-Jumbo" to "On Bad Verse".

I was struck by the comments of George Packer in his foreword to a collection of Orwell's narrative essays entitled *Facing Unpleasant Facts*. He writes:

"Essays seem to offer almost limitless room to improvise and experiment, and yet their very freedom makes them unforgiving of literary faults: sloppiness, vagueness, pretension, structural misshapenness, an immature voice, insular material, and the nearly universal plague of bad thinking are all mercilessly exposed under the spotlight in which the essayist stands alone onstage. There are no props, no sets, no other actors; the essayist is the existentialist of literature, and a mediocre talent will wear out his audience within a couple of paragraphs."

I leave the reader to judge whether I have avoided those very real faults. Thanks to those formative times I spent in the small alcove in the Harvard Book Store, it has been a stimulating, at times joyous, at times sobering experience.

Jolyon Nuttall
June 2018

Can You Cook?

JEAN DIED ON 27 FEBRUARY 2013. Next day the packers came to our home in Newlands in Cape Town. The day after, the removers arrived. By noon, as required, the house stood empty.

I drove ahead to our former weekend cottage in Kommetjie, near Cape Point, which we had decided to make our permanent base. The last items of furniture, together with sixty-two boxes of possessions, were offloaded by 4 p.m. With my daughter and my son, I watched the van disappear up the road.

Hester from across the street telephoned to say that flowers for my daughter had been delivered to her house earlier in the day. I said I would fetch them. She was waiting at her front door. She handed me the flowers: they were from Sarah's colleagues at Wits University. I told her Jean had died. She hugged me and we both cried.

As the afternoon turned to dusk, I was unpacking items in the kitchen. I looked up and saw Hester's husband, my good friend Eddie, leaning on the stable door. In the home, Eddie spoke Afrikaans but he always spoke English to me. I could see he was deeply disturbed.

"Jolyon," he said in Afrikaans, staring hard at me, "gaan jy stokalleen hier bly?"

I was taken aback by the starkness of the question.

"Ek weet nie, Eddie, maar ek gaan probeer."

For a long while, Eddie pondered in silence. Then he jabbed a finger at me and asked in English:

"Can you cook?"

Such was the profusion of things to attend to — meeting with undertakers, arranging a private cremation, organising a subsequent memorial gathering, sending and receiving messages, starting to unpack, stifling bouts of overwhelming grief — that it took me several days to understand what Eddie was getting at.

Then I realised that he was conveying the age-old conception that husbands are expected to die before their wives. After all, the statistics showed that women lived longer than men. And women, of course, did the cooking in the household. What Eddie was picturing before his eyes as he leaned on my stable door was a poor soul who had bucked convention and almost certainly didn't know how to boil an egg. Take Eddie. He could boil up the crayfish he had caught from his boat that morning, no problem there, in the same way that many white South African men fancy their skills at the braai. But that was it. Hester would prepare their meals as she had done through fifty years and more of marriage. That was how things were, the pattern of marriage.

Now, here before him was this neighbour of his who had been foolish enough to outlive his wife and broken the accepted sequence of things. What did he think he was about? Didn't he know what he was letting himself in for? Floundering about in that room of a house where men hardly ever crossed the threshold. Eddie's heart ached for him. It really was a pitiful fate to contemplate.

꘡

"YES, EDDIE, I CAN COOK."

꘡

What was that? He says he can cook. Hah, I wonder. We shall see. I bet it won't be long before he comes running over the road to Hester.

"Ah well, Jolyon, veels geluk."

 ⁓

I learned to cook long before I married. I faced a choice: eat baked beans from a tin or learn to cook. It wasn't so difficult. Perhaps you didn't face that option, Eddie. Perhaps your mother cooked for the family until you married. More likely, someone in the kitchen cooked – can you remember her name?

You know, Eddie, once you can cook, you cease to be dependent. You can be bold, adventurous, romantic. Take one example. There was this girl, you see, who touched my neck with her fingers, just above my collar, while we were dancing. When she laughed, it was like a warm gurgle. We had only just met but I knew I had to see her again.

So this is what I did, Eddie. I asked her to dinner. That afternoon, I drove to a farm in the Natal Midlands which had a river winding through it that was stocked with brown trout. I had about an hour before I would have to head home. Would the gods be with me? They just had to be, Eddie.

Not at first, though. Not after half an hour either – or forty-five minutes. Then, from under a bank, there was a swirl, and a take, and I had my trout.

I cooked it to perfection, Eddie, and served it with strips of bacon, the way my mother used to. My guest was astonished, in awe. Such unexpected enterprise and talent. So creative, such bold thinking. Later that evening, I kissed her and she laughed that deep gurgle of hers and kissed me back.

What do you think of that, Eddie? Simple, really, all I had to do was to learn to cook.

Life in Poufcastle

I FIND IT REALLY RATHER extraordinary that, in looking back over a long life, my mind and its memories keep returning to the four years from 1944 to 1947 that I spent with my family in the northern Natal town of Newcastle. I can conclude only that it is because they were so different from any of the times I had experienced before or after going there.

For my father — an ambitious person who since 1927 had taught English and Latin at Durban High School, one of the country's finest schools, known to everyone as DHS — promotion was long overdue. When the Second World War broke out in 1939, he had enlisted with the South African Artillery but was recalled for what were known as "essential services on the home front" until, finally, in 1944 he was able to take up the headmastership of Newcastle High School. He plunged into preparations for the new job with great energy and enthusiasm. Because the school was run on parallel medium lines, with English-speaking and Afrikaans-speaking children accommodated in their own classes, it was vital that he improve his Afrikaans for which there had been virtually no demand in Durban. This he did, working through Afrikaans grammar books and doing what he could to build his conversational skills through sessions with the master who taught Afrikaans at DHS.

One of his early disappointments occurred when we all arrived at Newcastle's railway station at the beginning of 1944. A senior master named Charles Beukes had been deputed to meet the new arrivals. Anxious to put his newly acquired Afrikaans to the test, my father, who was an avid flyfisherman, posed a question almost at once:

"Sê vir my, is daar forelle hier?"

Beukes, a friendly man who later did his best to teach my father how to play golf, looked puzzled. My father had to repeat his question. Suddenly the man's face lit up.

"O, bedoel Meneer trout?"

I sometimes think that things in Newcastle went downhill for my father from then on.

For my twin brother and me, however, it was a newfound paradise. For one thing, by coming to Newcastle, we had been released from boarding school in the village of Hillcrest, some thirty miles inland from Durban. We had been sent there at the age of eight because of the threat of Japanese submarines off the Natal coast. In the two years we had been there, we had contracted measles and chickenpox in quick succession and were lodged with other boys in the school's sanatorium, homesick and disoriented. Our parents visited us no more than three or four times because of petrol rationing, so we saw them only at school holidays.

For another, we city boys suddenly found ourselves transported to a new world in which the rural and the urban were interlaced. Properties were large and many of the town's citizens kept a horse and sheep and hens, and grew mealies and vegetables, and had orchards full of fruit trees. The town's roads, all of them gravel except the main Johannesburg–Durban road, which ran through the town, were generously wide and, in no time, we had acquired our own bikes and cycled at will in our neighbourhood. What's more, it quickly became apparent that the headmaster, die hoofonderwyser, was one of the four most important people in the town, with a status that commanded respect from all and sundry, so we felt a little important too. The other three were the magistrate (known as the Beak), the dominee, who lived opposite us and always had the newest and largest car in the town, and the doctor.

The Headmaster's House stood on two acres, one of which was undeveloped and wild and marvellous to explore. Our parents dubbed it the Wilderness, but for us it was a place where we could build a log shelter and have mock 'sleep-outs' and fight off hostile forces that tried to invade our territory. The house itself was large, high-ceilinged with spacious rooms and a verandah that ran round two sides of the house where we could roller-skate. Soon we had hens and ducks and pigeons. And, as we made friends among the boys at the school who came from neighbouring farms, we were invited out at weekends and went searching for remains of pottery in Bushmen's caves and fished for bluegill in the dams and found birds' eggs in nests under culverts.

Our first year was spent at the junior school and we passed our time there happily enough although there was a rough-and-tumble aspect to the play that we had to learn to roll with. I remember an irate Afrikaans-speaking parent rapping loudly on the front door of the Headmaster's House, carrying her son's blazer bearing a ripped pocket and claiming to my bewildered mother, whose Afrikaans was extremely limited, that we should have to pay for a new blazer because she certainly couldn't afford another. My brother and I denied all knowledge of the incident. The matter was finally smoothed over when my mother arranged to have the ripped pocket invisibly mended.

I think my mother used to dread a knock on the front door. On another occasion, she opened the door to find an obsequious farmer's wife standing there with a live, plump rooster under her arm which she duly handed over, entreating my mother to accept "this scrawny gift" as a welcome to the area.

For the next three years, we attended the senior school, completing Standards 5 and 6 as they then were (now Grades 7 and 8) in English medium and then, because we were young for our age group, repeating Standard 6 in the Afrikaans-medium class. This certainly improved our bilingualism, studying as we did geskiedenis and aardrykskunde. My mother taught us Latin at home in place of Engels.

My father's early enthusiasm gradually diminished as he found himself wrestling with unexpected challenges at the girls' hostel and parents from the platteland who came to plead that they could not afford to pay the paltry school fees — "Meneer, ek kan nie betaal nie." — and endless staffing and administrative concerns. As we turned to loving the town, he turned to hating it. To him, it became Poufcastle. The only occasions on which I saw him really happy were when the school terms ended and we were able to take the train to a farm in the Natal Midlands where he could fish for "forelle" to his heart's content. He would reserve a second-class compartment for the four of us, knowing full well that, although it could accommodate six, this was unlikely to happen. Just to make sure, however, he would give the conductor a handsome and quite unnecessary tip. The first stop was at Ballengeich, a coal mining settlement less than half an hour from Newcastle. At that point, my mother would be asked to produce the stuffed eggs, a delicacy she would make as part of the padkos for the journey, and my father would smile happily as he sat back in his seat, said "Goodbye, Poufcastle," and proceeded to devour more than his share.

His dislike for Newcastle was compounded when, on one awful day, I was sent to the Headmaster's Office with a note from the class teacher. I had been fooling around with my classmates during a music lesson, joining in a general shoving and pushing and pinching. The teacher, recently qualified and determined to maintain discipline, gave us a stern warning to behave. She turned back to the piano, only to hear further scuffles and giggles behind her. She swung round and her eye fell on me.

"That's it," I remember her saying as she sat down to write a note to the headmaster. The classroom was dead silent as I left and made my way to my father's office. He called, "Come in," only to leap from his chair when he saw me and the note I was carrying. I was trembling as I stood there.

"Oh, no, Jo," he stammered, "not you."

Oh, yes. There was nothing for it but for me to bend down and he whacked me three times, hard, on my posterior.

My father had this to say when recounting the experience in his family record called *Tales of Another Grandfather*:

"I knew all the staff would be agog, wondering whether the H.M. would let his son off. It was a trivial offence for which I would never have caned another boy but I couldn't and didn't let my own son off. Jo took it like a man and only said, 'Sorry, Dad' when it was over. I shut the door and wept. So did we all when we met as a family again at lunchtime."

I think he was generous to me. I too found it a humiliating experience which took some days to get over.

Newcastle gave us our first encounters with what were known as "poor whites". They were nearly all Afrikaans-speaking and lived mostly as bywoners (tenants) on district farms. I remember the lesson coming home to me after my brother and I had been selected for the Under-15 cricket team along with other teammates and were scheduled to play against schools in the region. It emerged that several of the boys in the team did not have "whites" (clothing, in this instance) to wear. One boy in particular appealed to my brother and me to go home with him and plead with his parents to make a plan. They were bywoners on a farm just outside the town. We cycled out there and were shocked when we saw the rundown farm building in which they lived. It became rapidly clear that there was no chance that the parents could afford the long, white trousers, the white shirt and the white sandshoes that made up the cricket "uniform", something we middle-class kids took for granted. I have no recollection of what happened thereafter but I can imagine how wretched that boy felt. Perhaps we all got together and lent him what was required. I hope so.

In the winter we played rugby, which, like cricket, required sports gear. On one particular Saturday, we were to play a side from the little town of Memel from across the border in the Orange Free State, as it then was. The Memel team took to the field barefoot but, when the time came for them to take a penalty in reach of the posts, a boot was sent for and their flyhalf slotted the kick without any trouble.

One of the major cultural events in Newcastle each year was the Schools Eisteddfod. All the music teachers in the town would prepare their pupils to sit the practicals before a select group of judges from other parts of the country. The star performers – those who achieved a gold, silver, perhaps even a bronze certificate – would then go forward to appear on stage in the Newcastle Town Hall before a packed audience of dignitaries, the teachers themselves, – nervously clutching their handbags – proud parents and other pupils.

When we arrived in Newcastle, my mother enrolled my brother and me as pupils of a Mrs Viljoen, who had been recommended to her. We would go to her house for lessons once a week and would be given keyboard exercises – arpeggios and the like – plus musical works to practise at home. These sessions took place before school. My brother, being an ardent fellow, would be first up for half an hour and then go off and feed the hens and the pigeons while I followed him at the piano.

In our second year, we must have been judged by Mrs Viljoen to have made sufficient progress to be entered in that year's round of judging for the Eisteddfod. We performed our pieces and did rather well, Michael getting a gold and I a silver. Thus we became eligible to play in the concert which climaxed the event. It all went off without a hitch and Mrs Viljoen exuded pride in being the music teacher of the headmaster's twins.

When the time came round again the following year, Mrs Viljoen's ambitions took a considerable leap. She decided that the twins should play a duet. From the very beginning, it was an unfortunate choice. For one thing, it upset our practice routine. Instead of one following the other, my brother and I now had to practise together, which meant that I had to rise earlier than I was accustomed to doing and this tended to put me in a foul temper. For another, the piece proved to be quite technically advanced compared with what we had played the year before. We soldiered on, however, with periodic outbursts of "Michael, you rat!" and "Jolyon, you clot!" when one or other of us made a mistake. In truth, we got to know the piece so well in the weeks before the Eisteddfod that we could almost play it with our eyes shut, or so we thought, and Mrs Viljoen judged us ready to play before the judges. Indeed, we were more than ready and performed with aplomb to gain a gold certificate. So we were duly entered for the grand finale.

Perhaps you can picture the scene on that evening. The dominee and his wife were seated next to the headmaster and his wife in the front row, along with the judges and the leading music teachers, including Mrs Viljoen. The winning pupils came on stage, performed, were applauded as they took a bow or a curtsey, and left, and so on. Then it was our turn. There were murmurs round the hall as the twins took up their positions at the piano and the word oulik (cute) was bandied about.

It did not go well. For some unaccountable reason, we got off to a false start, with either Michael beginning to play before I was quite ready or, in all probability, me starting off before he was ready. We were thus required to start again, a huge negative in the world of duets, and it threw us completely off our timing. Our progress through the piece that we could virtually play in our sleep became a nightmare and I reached the bottom of the first page and turned it to begin the second before Michael had got there. Chaos reigned as we stopped again, dug each other in the ribs, gathered ourselves and played stoically on until we reached the end. As we did so, I remember glancing down at Mrs Viljoen sitting in the front row. She had her hand over her downcast eyes. We stood up, gave a lightning quick bow and left the stage to a few muffled handclaps.

For our parents, it must have been untold agony and, for Mrs Viljoen, a cataclysmic disaster. My mother diplomatically withdrew us as pupils and we never saw the front or the back of an Eisteddfod again.

✢

To borrow a phrase from that master essayist George Orwell, "such, such were the joys" of life in Poufcastle. We all left at the end of the following year. My brother and I became boarders at Maritzburg College and my parents returned to Durban and thence to Pietermaritzburg. My father was elevated to the schools' inspectorate in the province and then as principal of the Natal Teachers' Training College, a post for which he was eminently qualified and which finally brought him professional fulfilment.

The Alan Paton I Knew

ALAN PATON FIRST FEATURED in my life when I was ten. It was in the mid-1940s. My father had just taken up the headmastership of Newcastle High School in northern Natal, a town that lay approximately halfway between Durban and Johannesburg.

One day my father announced that his friend from his university days, Alan Paton, and his son David were coming to spend the night with us, en route between the two cities. I remember being taken aback when they arrived on bicycles and I was agog when I learned that they were riding from Johannesburg to Durban, a total distance of over seven hundred kilometres. To a ten-year-old, that seemed an unthinkably long journey on a cycle. Even by car in those days it was not to be taken lightly, with portions of the road not yet tarred and with countless hills and valleys to be negotiated. Several punctures were almost certain. In any case, it was during the Second World War when there was severe petrol rationing and nearly everybody wanting to travel between the two cities took the train.

I remember a stocky, deeply suntanned and understandably weather-beaten figure pushing his bike up our drive, followed by a limping, bleeding, disconsolate sixteen-year-old obviously in need of what is known these days as TLC. David had come off his bike somewhere along the route, but it quickly became apparent that his father had no particular intention of mollycoddling him. It was as though he was saying, "You elected to ride with me, my boy, so don't expect me to feel sorry for you." In later years I was to learn that Alan Paton had a harsh streak in him – perhaps inherited in part from his father, who was said to be a mild man outside the home but a tyrant within it. Certainly, on that late afternoon in Newcastle, he came across as a tough disciplinarian. It was left to my mother to patch up David as best she could. On the following day he continued the next leg of the journey by train while his father rode on alone.

I carried this impression of Paton with me in

all the years during which I encountered him. It has made me wonder, in fact, who the real Paton was and which side of his persona drove him to accomplish what he did. Whatever it was, it must have taken some tremendous inner resolve that may not always have been apparent.

Little did I know it at the time but Paton was within three years of writing *Cry, the Beloved Country*, which took the world by storm and freed him to become a fulltime writer. To me, at that first encounter, he was an extremely intense person with a clipped voice, expressive eyebrows and pursed mouth, and a wry sense of humour. When he laughed, which he did increasingly as the evening with us progressed, his whole body shook.

It was clear to me that he had a close bond with my parents and with my father in particular. They had come through university in Pietermaritzburg together, Alan two years my father's senior, and had forged what I was later to call, in my book about their relationship, a literary friendship. They soaked themselves in English poetry and prose in all their forms. Paton was to write in the first volume of his autobiography, *Towards the Mountain*, years later:

"... it was with Neville Nuttall that I made endless forays into literature. After an evening at his lodgings or at my home, we would walk back together to the cemetery in Commercial Road, and then would sit in the little arched building among the graves for another hour or more. It was Shakespeare, Milton, Wordsworth, Coleridge, Keats, Shelley, Byron, Tennyson, Browning … we read the war poets, Wilfred Owen, Wilfrid Gibson, Julian Grenfell and of course Rupert Brooke … indeed I cannot now remember all that we read."

That evening in Newcastle became filled with nostalgia and banter and the quoting of their favourite passages from literature. The two talked late into the night in the comfortable Headmaster's House.

Paton at the time was well ensconced as principal of Diepkloof Reformatory on the East Rand, a post he had taken up with the title of Warden in 1935 at the youthful age of thirty-two. In his years there, he had changed the place from what was, in effect, a prison for juveniles to an institution with a diminished focus on detention and locked cell doors and punishment and greater emphasis on one that provided measures for genuine reform and opportunity in the way it was run. In doing so, he demonstrated strict discipline, outwardly, and deep compassion, inwardly, two distinct sides of a coin and further clues to his persona.

In later years, I learned that, although in many ways the more literary of the two (Paton graduated in maths and science), my father held the view that Paton would make the more lasting impact, in one way or another, in his time – and had said so in a letter to Paton a few years before Alan's visit to Newcastle. His prediction came true with the publication of *Cry, the Beloved Country*.

On 15 February 1948, Paton sent my father one of the first six author's copies the publishers had dispatched to him. That copy remains in our family today. The success of the book is history.

George Orwell, in his 1946 essay "Why I Write", spoke for many of his fellow authors when he said: "Writing a book is a horrible, exhausting struggle, like a long bout of some painful illness. One could never undertake such a thing if one were not driven on by some demon whom we can neither resist nor understand."

I do not believe that this was the case at all in the writing of *Cry, the Beloved Country*. It simply poured out of Paton as though a cork had been pulled from a bottle. But it certainly applied to the writing of his second novel, *Too Late the Phalarope*. Given the acclaim with which his first novel had been received, it was not surprising that pressure built on him to produce the second. With his wife Dorrie, he had settled in the small resort of Anerley on the Natal South Coast to pursue a career as a writer. Now a boy of sixteen, I went with my family to visit them there. He was the same Alan Paton, the mix of gruff comments and bursts of humour. Fame had not gone to his head. But it became clear during our visit that his Muse – so vibrant in the writing of *Cry* – was not stirring. He was to write to his friend Mary Benson in London at that time: "I haven't a single idea about a book ... freedom has gone to my head. I do almost nothing."

By 1951, however, his writer's block had cleared and the second novel was under way. It came with the torment described by Orwell. Set in the town of Ermelo in what was then the Eastern Transvaal, it depicted the lives of Afrikaners grappling with private issues in the face of a strict law forbidding interracial sexual relationships. Many critics saw the work as a modern-day Greek tragedy. My parents were visiting Britain in that year and they met up with Alan in London. The question of a title for the book came up and my father was to record in later years: "One day at his flat in London he handed us a bit of paper with *Too Late the Phalarope* written on it and that we all three decided was the right title. This bit of paper is in our copy of the *Phalarope* – also a first edition."

Paton had the satisfaction of having proved that he was not a "one-book man", but a small controversy arose over the subject of the title. The phalarope is a seabird which nests inland. Doubts were expressed, however, that it had ever been seen in Ermelo. This led to a delightful exchange of poems between the two men, written in Paton's case on a postcard and my father's response on a small writing pad. After my father's death, I found them both (in my father's case, a pencil copy of the original sent to Paton) in a cardboard box with other exchanges between the two. Paton was first up with the following piece of deliberate doggerel, dated 12 September 1951, from Anerley:

Once in the Tavern of the Seas
The penguin and the phalarope
Did meet and of their joy imbibe
Some real Cape Province dope.

Thus quite unusually they spoke
With forthright tongues and free
And said what never they'd have said
Just ordinarily.

I'm sick and tired, the penguin said,
Of ice and snow, in future
I'm spending all my winter vacs
Up there at Cape St Lucia.

And then the gentle phalarope
He too was sick of ice and snow

And thought he'd spend his winter vac
Up there at Ermelo.

At Ermelo, the penguin said,
My God you go too far
My God we are both ocean birds
Let's stick to what we are.

And who are you, said phalarope,
My God sir, who are you?
I'll go to any bloody place
To make that book come true.

My father's undated response reads:

I love the gentle phalarope,
I love him more and more,
Putting the penguin in his place
Upon the sanding shore.
I love his quick and nimble wit,
His quirk of humour rare
But, most of all, his will to roam,
To travel anywhere.
He'll go to any bloody place
On any bloody date
And, always willing to oblige,
He'll even come too late.
So trust the phalarope, my son,
And let him come and go

And all the world will chant his name
And never even know.

～

I spent two years, between July 1956 and June 1958, working as a journalist in London. On my return to South Africa, I was shaken when I realised the extent to which apartheid was tightening its grip on the country, ten years after the National Party had come to power. None of the parliamentary parties in opposition offered any acceptable political home to me and I turned instead to the fledgling Liberal Party, which espoused initially a qualified franchise for all races but, from the 1960s, was to move to the doctrine of "one man, one vote" — utter anathema to all but a tiny percentage of the white population. The president of the Liberal Party, drawn reluctantly but almost inescapably into politics from his writer's domain, was Alan Paton.

As a working journalist, I kept my membership of the Liberal Party a closely guarded secret, but I have no doubt my conservative news editor was aware where my sentiments lay. Be that as it may, it was not long before I was assigned to cover a meeting of the Liberal Party which was to be held in a hall in the little town of Camperdown, some twenty-five kilometres from Pietermaritzburg.

I quickly realised on arrival why a small venue had been chosen. The audience numbered no more than twenty and at least half of them, by my estimate, were party members who had travelled from the university campus in Pietermaritzburg to attend. There were three blacks, one of whom I had brought to the meeting. At the very back sat the representatives of the Security Branch of the South African Police.

It was my first exposure to Paton in his role as public persona in what was ominous and dangerous terrain. The inner steel in him was on display. He opened the meeting in his clipped voice with what was to become his hallmark greeting on the political stage: "Ladies and gentlemen, and members of the Special Branch."

There was a titter of laughter from the audience and some turned round to peer at the unwelcome intruders. Paton spoke firmly and well, attacking the regime and urging representation for all races in the political structures of the country. I filed my report for the following day's editions. After a thorough search, I found two paragraphs on page fourteen of the newspaper.

In the years that followed, many Liberal Party members, and particularly its leadership, were detained and placed under banning orders and persecuted. Alan himself had his passport confiscated and his home searched. But he stuck it out until 1968 when the government passed an act which banned parties from having a multiracial membership. The Liberal Party was forced to choose between disbanding and going underground. In that year, it chose to disband.

Paton continued to write and he did not sever his links with his close friends, although there were some who were jealous of his fame as a writer and critical of his politics. He continued to love the outdoors, the hills and streams he longed for when he was away. I remember joining my parents and the Patons – Alan and Dorrie – in 1962 for a weekend at a Parks Board camp at the foot of Giants Castle in the Drakensberg. Alan and my father attempted to resurrect the old times, skirting politics and teasing each other. But Dorrie was unwell, worn down by emphysema, which was to claim her life in 1969, and it over-shadowed their efforts. I remember travelling in the back seat of the Patons' car at the end of that weekend with a silent Alan hunched over the wheel. He was determined, I learned, to get home for his reading hour from 6 p.m. to 7 p.m., a sacrosanct period in his day.

The death of Dorrie left a huge hole in Paton's life and before the year was out he had married again, to his secretary, Anne Hopkins. A highly efficient person of British descent, she had set about bringing order from the moment he employed her to the messy shambles into which his workaday life had descended. She also erected a barrier between him and the numerous people who plagued him with requests for interviews or to speak at their functions or to read their manuscripts.

There were two sets of casualties from her self-imposed role to protect him from the outside world as she saw it. First, Paton's sons, in particular Jonathan, the younger of the two, shocked no doubt by their father's swift remarriage, fell out with her, as so often happens in similar circumstances in other families. Jonathan and his wife Margaret had always been close to him, but the relationship deteriorated to the extent that Paton cut Jonathan out of his will.

The other casualties were his close friends, some of them lifelong, including my parents. My father, who had become used to telephoning Alan on occasion, found himself repeatedly blocked. He found it infuriating.

To what extent was Paton aware of this? I have reason to believe he was uncomfortable about it, at the very least. In the early 1980s, I was invited to dinner at the home of a close colleague of mine who was editor of the *Sunday Tribune*. His name was Ian Wyllie. He and Paton, who lived nearby, had formed a firm friendship and every Wednesday evening Alan came, on his own, to dinner. This was one such evening. Wyllie kept a fine selection of wine and whiskies, which the celebrated author consumed with gusto. He was in ebullient form, more so than at any other time I could remember. It was as though he was relishing every moment of a newfound sense of freedom. I was in stitches most of the evening as the cut-and-thrust of the conversation rollicked along. As always, there was a difference at some point in the evening over the meaning of a word. A dictionary was sent for and the controversy settled. If ever there was a more apt adherence than that evening to the adage "Eat, drink and be merry — for tomorrow we die", I have yet to find one.

My father died in 1983 and Alan spoke movingly at his funeral, recounting Neville's generosity to him at all times, his lack of jealousy and envy at Paton's success as a writer when it was thought that it might be Nuttall who would produce *the* great novel. Paton himself lived for another five years and, when he died in 1988, he left behind a substantial body of work that has secured his place in the canon of South African writers.

Looking back now, I remember, from my first encounter with him, the hard streak, the tough, resilient characteristic, part inherited perhaps in his genes, that lurked within him, an underlay to the free spirit and quirky humour that emerged when he could truly relax. And it has become clear to me that it was this combination that saw him through a multitude of challenges in his life. There were times when that mental toughness was vital in the various roles he fulfilled, as writer, as prison reformer, as politician hounded by the Security Police. There were times when it spilled over into his domestic life. But his other side, his love of words, his boundless curiosity, his mischievous sense of humour, was the balancing dimension without which he would have been a lesser person.

Sundays

S UNDAYS AT BOARDING SCHOOL in Pietermaritzburg, a city full of schools and churches, followed a pattern inherited from our colonial past. After breakfast, an affair of porridge and overcooked scrambled eggs made from egg powder, we were required to get ready for church. At ten o'clock, in full school uniform complete with straw bashers, we set out in crocodile fashion for the morning service in the centre of the city at the various denominations into which religion had been carved. The list included Anglicans, Methodists, Presbyterians, Christian Scientists, Baptists, Congregationalists, Roman Catholics and a 'Holy Roller' or two.

At the start of the lengthy walk to the city centre,

we formed a single crocodile from the school, down to the park on the banks of the Msunduzi River and up a steep incline of steps until we reached the entry point of our destination. Thereafter, the cluster of rowdy schoolboys started to fan out and thin out as boys peeled off to their respective churches. The first to leave us were the Christian Scientists: they entered a substantial red-brick building that looked to me, I remember, more like an administrative centre than a church. Then we lost some Baptists and Congregationalists and a few Presbyterians. The Catholics (not many of them) made their way off somewhere and I can't remember what happened to the Holy Rollers, leaving two remaining groups, the Methodists and Anglicans, by far the largest contingents. My twin brother and I belonged to the former and the Anglicans pushed on to their final destination.

Services started at eleven o'clock. What cheered us greatly was the knowledge that, at the end of the service, provided we had lodged details with the boarding master on duty at the school before departing, we were free from the time the service ended until roll call at 6 p.m. in the school quad. For my brother and me, this meant that we could head for my parents' home – for they had moved to the city after we had enrolled as boarders and it was decided we should stay on – where my mother would have a Sunday roast with all the trimmings ready for her hungry sons.

The Methodists were extremely proud of their singing and the morning service was punctuated with what seemed to us to be an inordinate number of lengthy hymns, most of them written by Charles Wesley, who, with his brother John, was the founder of the Wesleyan, later Methodist, denomination that broke away from the Church of England and became part of the Nonconformist Movement, a historical fact of which we were only dimly aware. As Nonconformists, we were given to understand that Methodist churches had been stripped of the regalia and the pomp and ceremony of the C of E churches and restored to simpler exteriors and interiors. The order of service, we gathered, was less formal and far less structured than that of the Anglicans down the road. This gave the ministers who conducted the services the freedom to make up their own prayers rather than follow those set down in the Anglican order of service and, what was more relevant to those of us anxious to be free when the service ended, to preach a sermon of any length that they felt the occasion required. Taken together, from the hymn singing to the closing prayers, this meant that we seldom emerged from morning service until 12.20 p.m. and sometimes, after queuing up to shake the minister's hand, nigh on 12.30.

Our Anglican school friends, out sharp at 12

noon from their services, or so they said, were aghast. We viewed their claims with suspicion until, one Sunday, we were persuaded to attend a morning service at St Peter's Church where a priest by the name of the Reverend Angus Milne conducted the proceedings. I remember having a slight feeling of guilt that we were doing this without notifying either the school or our parents. However, this was assuaged not only when we emerged sharp at 12 noon but also because both of us had found the sermon, drawn as it was from the earlier Gospel readings, to be precise and interesting.

So it came about that, without any obstacles placed in our way by our parents, in particular my father, who was an ardent Methodist, my mother having come from Presbyterian stock, we became Anglicans.

And thereby hangs a tale ...

We discovered some years later, as our interest in our ancestors grew, that our lineage was littered with men of the cloth, on my father's paternal and maternal side, and on my mother's paternal side. Three names—all straight out of the Old Testament — began to punctuate the answers to the questions with which we plied my father as we tried to put the pieces of this lineage together: Enos, Ezra and Ebenezer. Three brothers, Nuttalls all, of whom Ezra was my father's grandfather and, although we never knew him, our great-grandfather. My father's information about his antecedents had come in part from his mother but mostly from "Aunt Ada", more formally addressed as Lady Lamb, whose husband had been knighted for his work at what was then Tanganyika. Subsequent research has shown that Aunt Ada's memories were tinged with romanticism, but no matter. She was correct in much of her information. The father of the three brothers, James Nuttall, was a lay preacher in Harrogate, a spa town in North Yorkshire, and — lo and behold — all three sons followed in their father's footsteps.

Enos was to achieve high office in the hierarchy of the Church of England: having been sent to Jamaica as an unordained missionary, he was ordained in 1866 and subsequently consecrated as Bishop of Jamaica by the Archbishop of Canterbury in St Paul's, London, in 1880 and, in 1893, became the Archbishop of the West Indies.

Ebenezer, rumoured incorrectly by Aunt Ada to have become the editor of *The Church Times*, attended Worcester College, Oxford, and served as deacon and then priest in the Church of England in his home country.

What of Ezra? He broke ranks and came with his wife to what was then Natal as a missionary of the Wesleyan Church, first to Verulam and then to Edendale, just outside Pietermaritzburg, where he established a school and training college for Africans which was called the Nuttall Institution. Eventually, the couple with their five children moved to Durban and lived at the Wesleyan parsonage in Aliwal Street. Ezra was twice the president of the Conference in the Methodist Church, its highest post. Referred to as an "ecclesiastical statesman", he was the equivalent of an archbishop in the Anglican Church he had abandoned.

My father's father, Edgar Edge Nuttall — known as Eddie — was the eldest of the children. He married Ethel Wynne, whose father, William Wynne — believe it or not — was a Methodist minister. He too had been sent by his church to South Africa, in part because he was virtually under sentence of death from TB. The dry air certainly improved his condition, for he lived until he was seventy-seven. He moved around the Circuit until he and his family came to Durban and set up home in the imposing Methodist manse in Norfolk Road. William Wynne, too, became president of the Methodist Conference, another virtual archbishop in the family.

My father's father died of meningitis in his early thirties and so his devastated wife Ethel, by then the mother of my father, aged four, and a daughter in her arms and left virtually penniless, was obliged to move back into the family manse.

So William Wynne, a strict disciplinarian and strong personality, became the father figure in my own father's life until his death in 1920. My father used to tell us in dramatic terms how Grandfather Wynne was conducting the service at the Musgrave Methodist Church, with his mother playing the organ, when he had a sudden heart attack in the pulpit and died at home without regaining consciousness. This seemed to me at the time the dream way, the Hollywood way, for a distinguished man of the cloth to end his life.

I have yet more to add to my tale. My father married Ethel Lucy Hewitt, whom he met when they were students – he four years her senior – at university in Pietermaritzburg. And Lucy Hewitt was the daughter of the Rev. Dr Edward Hewitt, DD, a Presbyterian minister, adding yet more emphasis on the ecclesiastical side of our family. Although he was born in Ulster, he grew up and was educated in Scotland and spoke with a Scottish burr. He came to South Africa with British troops during the Anglo-Boer War. He married Ethel Cowley Grice, of a distinguished Natal family. A scholarly man, the Rev. Dr was very absent-minded and would meet his own children in the street and look at them vaguely as if he didn't know who they were. He loved to go to auctions and bought all sorts of things the family didn't need and couldn't really afford. To his wife's horror, he also acquired from a salesman knocking on his front door at home the 1911 edition of the *Encyclopaedia Britannica*, which ran to many volumes and which is still in our family to this day. He would proudly demonstrate its superb physical attributes by holding up one of the substantial volumes by a single page, said to be made of the finest India paper. Perhaps while musing on some esoteric subject, he was knocked down by a car near his home and died from his injuries, one of the earliest street accidents in Durban.

～

Little did my brother and I or our parents or any member of the wider family know on that Sunday when we entered St Peter's Church for the first time that one of us would go on to become Bishop of Pretoria, then Bishop of Natal and Dean of the Province, the number two to the Archbishop of Cape Town. However, if the family – gifted with prescience – had been asked which of the two it would be, there is no doubt they would have known it was Michael. I could have told them from the age of about five.

And so it all went full circle from those breakaway days in the nineteenth century to the latter part of the twentieth.

Hallelujah!

Note: My parents retired to a small farm on the banks of the Umzimkulu River just outside Underberg in Natal. There was no Methodist Church there. The choice was the Congregational Church in Underberg or the Anglican Church in neighbouring Himeville. They chose the Anglican Church and in due course my father was asked to become a supplementary priest attached to the Himeville parish. He filled the role with devotion but, deep down, I knew, he remained a Methodist at heart. For one thing, those Anglicans couldn't sing.

Calf Love

THE MOST DELICIOUS, YET equally agonising, times of my life were those early encounters with the opposite sex. They would suddenly flare up with the kind of passion that would cause me to toss and turn all night and then, like a fireworks rocket, burn out and bring me tumbling back to earth. Until the next time.

My very first encounter, however, was somewhat different. I was not the instigator and it took me by surprise. It happened like this. For many years, we used to go as a family of four at Christmas to a guest farm in the Dargle valley in the Natal Midlands. By the time I hit my mid-teens, I had become nearly as enthusiastic a flyfisherman as my trout-mad father and spent many hours each day on the banks of the upper Umgeni River, which flowed through the farm, in pursuit of the wily browns that thrived there.

Then there came a Christmas holiday when another family of four arrived to sample the pleasures of farm life. Included in the family were two teenage girls – and pretty ones, too. My twin brother was less enthusiastic about fishing and, hey presto, I returned from a long day on the river to find a twinkle in his eye and a matching twinkle in the eye of the younger one of the glamorous daughters. This left me and the even more beautiful elder daughter twiddling our thumbs, so to speak.

One day the spirited younger daughter came to me and said I should ask my brother why he was "so slow". I passed on the message with some glee. Put out by its contents, my brother took immediate action later in the evening.

Christmas passed with feasting and celebration and then came New Year's Eve. Every year, the local farming community held a dance in a hall in a tiny village called Boston, about forty kilometres away. My brother and I, along with other boarders at our school, had been going to dance classes in the school's dining hall during the year. We had no partners and so we had learned various steps with our arms held up at shoulder height. As we made our way in two cars along the dusty farm roads to Boston, I felt confident that I could invite the beautiful elder daughter to have the first dance with me.

It was a disaster. The gulf between simulated dancing and the real thing proved to be enormous. I trod on her toes and, as importantly, on her fancy dancing shoes. I stumbled about in growing embarrassment until mercifully the music ended and I could disappear into a distant corner of the hall.

As the evening passed, I began to look about me. Sitting alone on an upright chair against the wall was a pretty, young country girl with a red ribbon in her hair. I plucked up sufficient courage to ask her to dance. Suddenly, a miracle occurred. I found I could do all those fancy steps they had taught us at school. I became ever more fluent with the young lass in my arms. I knew I had found my level. There came the last dance and the girl with the red ribbon and I danced cheek to cheek, and wished each other a "happy New Year" and a "see you next year", and off she went with her parents to their district farm.

It was time to pile into our cars and head home. I found myself in the back seat along with my brother and his girl and, next to me, the glamorous elder daughter whom I had barely had the courage to address during the evening. We set off. But while we were at the dance a mighty storm had broken over the Inhlosane mountain range. We had travelled about ten kilometres when our car began to slither in the mud and then skidded across the road and stuck fast up to the running board. The more the farmer tried to get out of the mud, the deeper we went in. The other car had managed to get through and was out of sight, oblivious of our fate. There was nothing for it: he had to walk to the nearest farm to get help.

It had turned cold and we nestled down in the back seat. I remember feeling rather sleepy after the heady events of the evening and, turning towards the beautiful elder daughter, lowered my head on to her shoulder. It seemed that my awful performance on the dance floor was forgotten for, after a few moments, she bent over and kissed me. I have never forgotten that moment.

Needless to say, I spent the rest of the holiday doing a great deal less fishing than usual. And later that year, although she was at university, she came to the school dance with me and all my finesses came right.

❧

It was in the July holidays of that year that a school friend of ours invited my brother and me to spend ten days with him and his family in the sugarcane town of Amatikulu in Natal and to play in the annual Eshowe tennis tournament. This opened a whole new world to us, competitive tennis during the day and a social whirl of parties and dances in the evenings. As far as the tennis was concerned, we played in the singles, the doubles and the mixed doubles. The twins were teamed together in the doubles and, somewhat to our surprise, we won. The mixed doubles were a fun event during which I met a wonderful bubbly girl, the daughter of a prosperous sugarcane farmer, and we became an "item" for the rest of the tournament. Every small town or village in the district took turns to hold a "social", all of which proved to be hilarious evenings with a riotous range of dances. The bubbly girl and I became greatly involved and the passion flared between us.

When we returned to our schools, she and I wrote to each other at least three times a week, our outpourings escalating steadily from "Dearest" to "Darling" to "My dearest darling" and from "Lots of love" to "Tons of love" to "All my love". The fireworks rocket was exploding in the sky, sending out long sparklers of jewelled light.

Then, after a couple of months, almost imperceptibly at first, the depth of our passion began to subside until it came to the point when I wrote to say I thought we should end the affair but that I would always remember her, and thank you and *blah blah*. The following day, there came a letter from her — obviously written on the same day as I had written mine — saying precisely the same thing. All I could bring myself to do was to write back, saying, "Great minds think alike."

꒰꒱

The following July, we were invited back to defend our boys' doubles crown. Without hesitation, we accepted. It was all as much fun as the previous year had been, and this time I fell for a stunning girl whom I had hardly noticed the year before. Her name was Wendy and, as the social round gathered momentum, so did the degree of our involvement. She was a joy to be with and I was walking on air to have won her heart. Then a serious blow fell. It was the turn of Amatikulu, our home base, to hold a dance, which, unlike some of the other events, was for parents and players alike. Wendy's parents, who farmed just outside the nearby village of Gingindlovu (referred to commonly as Ging), learned that there would probably be alcohol available at the dance and forbade her to attend, although they themselves intended to. She told me she would have to stay at home on the farm. I was devastated.

The evening of the dance came. I went along with my brother and our friend, who were feeling very complacent because their partners were at the dance. For an hour or so I stood around in the crowded hall and then, on an impulse, I left and went down to the main road. I had been there for no more than a few minutes when a Land Rover came along with two fishermen returning from a late outing. I thumbed a lift and they picked me up. In no time I was spinning along the road to Ging, feeling very bucked with myself. The turn-off to the farm was just outside the village and they dropped me there. With my heart beating, I made my way up to the farmhouse and knocked on the door. Wendy opened it and, when she saw me there, she gave a gasp, followed by a cry of delight. She couldn't get over what I had done and, as it sank in, neither could I.

We talked and talked, and then she put on some music and we had our dance after all. It was bliss and the time passed in a warm haze. It was not until I glanced at my watch that I realised I had better start my journey back to base. By base, I meant the house in which we were staying. My plan was to hitch a lift back to Amatikulu, reach the house and get into bed before my brother and our friend and his parents arrived.

After a fond farewell and a joint pact to keep my visit a secret, I made my way down to the main road. As the minutes passed, the awful reality hit me: there were unlikely to be any cars on the road at that time of night. There was nothing for it

but to start to run — all of five kilometres. Run
I did, with growing panic in my heart because I
knew that, if all was discovered, I would be in deep
disgrace. I suppose I had the fitness and energy
of youth, and the exhilaration of the evening, to
assist me. I ran until my head was pounding as
much as my heart. I reached the house at fifteen
minutes before midnight, found an open window
and fell into bed as fast as I could, feigning sleep.

Soon I heard voices, and then my brother and
our friend came into the bedroom.

"Ah," I heard my brother say, "I told you he'd
be here."

"Poor guy," said our friend, "he must have
been really sad."

Starting Out

IT WAS THE PRACTICE AT Maritzburg College in my years there for our English master to set us every second Friday a topic on which we were required to write an essay over the weekend for submission on Monday. He would choose graphic idioms like *Out of the fat into the fire* or *It never rains but it pours* or, on one occasion, drawing from Shakespeare, *All's well that ends well.* His objective was to try to get us to use our imaginations and develop a writing style in the process that would result in gripping narratives. One of my efforts was returned to me with no more than an average mark and a note which read, "This essay is full of journalese."

Little was he to know that this was to lead me to my chosen career. Ignoring the derogatory connotation of his remark, I became fired up with the idea that I would become a journalist. I informed my parents accordingly. I am not sure whether they were amused or bemused but I think they were certainly pleased that I had settled on some sort of direction for the years ahead.

I had no idea about how to proceed, but this took shape during the Christmas holidays at the end of my last year at school. My family and a family from Durban used to go regularly to the same guest farm in the Natal Midlands. One evening around the large dinner table, I overheard the husband from the other family say to my father (they were both called Neville):

"Well, Neville, what are your boys going to do when they leave school?"

"They are both heading for university, Neville."

"And after that?"

"Jolyon thinks he would like to become a journalist."

"Well, Neville, he'd better come and spend a couple of weeks in our newsroom before the university term starts."

Unbeknown to me until then, the other Neville was the general manager of the leading afternoon newspaper in Durban. I did as he suggested and I was hooked at once. When I was asked to write a caption for a photograph and it was duly published, my pride knew no bounds. I had been there two weeks when the King of England, George VI, died. The news broke at midday. I watched, astonished, as that day's issue was transformed in a matter of an hour or two and a special edition was on the streets by 3.30 p.m.

Three years passed. I obtained my degree, having shaped it with subjects that seemed appropriate for journalism, and reported for duty at the same newspaper where the promise of a job had been kept. Several of the reporters had been at the very start of their careers when I spent those two weeks in the newsroom before going on to university. Now, I quickly became aware, they were often writing front-page stories and had adopted that cynical air that journalists like to project.

I must confess that I was taken aback when my first two tasks were to check the aircraft movements in and out of the city each day, for publication in the "What's On" column, and to compile the daily weather report. To complete this second task, I had to ring the Met Office and enter on a blank sheet the details that the voice at the other end gave me. These included the highest and lowest temperatures forecast for the following day, the rainfall figures if any, the times of the high and low tides and a number of other details. When I rang, the same person answered each day. He spoke with a very strong guttural accent. I suspect he was German. To begin with, my outwardly simple and rather humiliating task became a nightmare. I constantly had to ask him to repeat the statistics he had given me. When he had done this three times, I had to write down what I thought he had said. The readers of the newspaper must have been extremely puzzled and probably infuriated if they were fishermen or surfers, when they found, for example, that high tide did not occur at the time printed in the weather panel.

My initial difficulties were compounded by the noise that surrounded me in the newsroom. There was a constant hubbub of telephones ringing, reporters shouting down the line to their callers, typewriters clacking and the news editor calling out for feedback from his staff.

Gradually, however, I adapted to both my German friend's accent and the newsroom clatter, and I learned my first and lasting lesson in journalism: get the facts right and only thereafter add the bells and whistles. The news editor who started me on the aircraft movements and the weather panel knew a thing or two. He loved to say:

"It doesn't matter how good your story is, if you get a person's initials or surname or age wrong, you've blown it."

I loved the variety of assignments that came my

way in the newsroom as my expertise mounted. The news editor would pounce on me as I arrived at work:

"Jol" – he always called me Jol – "there's been a tornado that's swept over the Drakensberg. It's caused huge damage. There's a plane waiting at the airport. Get going with Laurie [the photographer assigned to fly with me]. I want a bird's eye report."

or

"Jol, there are two doctors in Greytown who have been taking out the appendix of everyone in town. There's an inquiry starting. I want you there for as long as it lasts."

or

"So-and-so's died. Please cover the funeral. There'll be lots of tributes."

Trouble was I never knew what clothes to wear to work. If I came in a suit, appropriate to cover a funeral, I would get sent to the North Pier because a fisherman had been swept off by a freak wave and I would get drenched. Or, if I came more casually dressed, I would be sent to a Rotary lunch where some big shot was speaking. On one such occasion, I found a Yale key in my blancmange, which made a juicy side panel for my story.

I learned to keep my eyes open. One day I was standing in for the shipping reporter, walking along the quayside eyeing the ships tied up in the harbour, when I did a double-take. Were my eyes deceiving me? I retraced my steps, looking up at the stern and then the bow of a trawler from foreign parts. No, my eyes were not. The ship had two names, one in front, one in the rear. I went on board and cornered the captain. He was taken aback and couldn't explain it. So I filed my story: the ship with two names.

"Nice one, Jol," the news editor said.

It turned out the trawler had recently been repainted and a stevedore had made a mistake with the spelling. I took as much satisfaction from the little stories as from the page leads I got. And research used to show that the little stories were often more widely read than the ones splashed all over the page.

One of my very first "little" stories was a single-paragraph appeal for blankets from the Child Welfare Society during a particularly cold spell in winter. My second was a two-paragraph story the next day recording that there had been an overwhelming response to the appeal.

In this way, and from many other examples, I learned the power of words. Correctly used, they could be forces for good. Distorted, they could be utterly destructive. Although my life has led me in many directions, the wordsmith in me has remained my ultimate resource. And I attribute much of this to those aircraft movements and that weather report.

On Boiling an Egg

I T IS A COMMONPLACE SAYING that someone is so incompetent when it comes to cooking that he or she cannot so much as boil an egg. Such a statement grossly underestimates the difficulties — and even disasters — that can occur when embarking on such a venture.

Take my father. His only contribution in the culinary field when I was young was to undertake the boiling of eggs for our Sunday supper. The poor man went through paroxysms of agony every week when executing this task. He knew that a soft-boiled egg required three and a half minutes immersed in a pot of boiling water. On the face of it, this was a simple enough operation. One would have thought that all it required was a reliable wristwatch. If only life had been so easy ...

His problem — and hence his agony — flowed from the harsh fact that, as soon as he lowered the four eggs into the pot, the water went off the boil. What to do? When exactly should he start timing the three and a half minutes required? From the point the water came back to the boil, which seemed the obvious answer, or should it be earlier on the basis that a certain amount of cooking must have taken place from the moment the eggs were put in the pot? It should be remembered, too, that the first egg to be lowered into the boiling water had been in longer than the fourth egg.

He knew that failure lay ahead if, in fact, the fourth egg — assuming he could still identify it — was removed first and was not much more than coddled and was bound to be dubbed "slimy" by his cruel sons. Or, worse, if the first egg was removed last, it could have reached the undesirable state of being hard-boiled and, therefore, declared inedible.

He would hop around the kitchen floor like a cat on hot bricks while the agonising process continued. In the event, more often than not, the fates were kind to him because the said three and a half minutes proved to allow a slight degree of flexibility on either side.

However, the condition of each egg could not be confirmed until it had been placed in its eggcup and opened with a teaspoon. We would all peer into our respective eggs to see if they were indeed in the condition in which we wanted to eat them. If they were, he would settle back with a proud expression on his face as if to say, "Well, it's easy when you know how."

On one successful evening, he even went so far as to declare: "I could be the king's egg-boiler."

But deep down, no doubt, he would think to himself that there was a whole precious week ahead until he had to do it again.

A Summer in New York

IN 1961 AT THE AGE OF TWENTY-SEVEN I was seconded
by my South African newspaper company to its
New York bureau for a year. My first two weeks in
Manhattan were the loneliest in my life and the
next fifty were the best. And, of those fifty, four in
mid-summer — a hot, steamy, grumpy period for
most New Yorkers — stand out in my memory as
the most remarkable. All because of Lewis Nkosi.

Lewis was the closest to a budding genius in
the world of writing that I have ever met. Two
years younger than me, he and I encountered
each other at Harvard University in Cambridge,
Mass., during a weekend visit I made to see a
South African friend who was studying there (and
to walk the hallowed Yard). We were at a cocktail

party for visiting scholars. Amid much mingling, I came face to face with a slim, youthful figure with a bulging stare, flashing eyes and an aura of brightness about him. I knew of Lewis Nkosi only through what I had read in the press: that, as a reporter for *Drum* magazine, a vibrant, bold and brave publication launched in the fifties as – to use his own subsequent description – "a symbol of the new African", he had been awarded a coveted Nieman Fellowship in journalism to study at Harvard. But, in order to take it up, he had been obliged to leave South Africa on an exit permit, which prevented his return to his own country. I remember thinking what an iniquitous imposition that was on a person's birthright.

Here before me now was the victim, who showed not the faintest sign of being sorry for himself. On the contrary, he exuded nervous energy and humour. By the time the encounter ended, I had established that he would be coming to New York in the summer and I had invited him to look me up – and stay with me for a while if he wished while he found lodgings. I had been fortunate enough to sub-let a spacious first-floor apartment in the heart of Greenwich Village, just off Washington Square, from a United Nations staffer who had been sent – irony of ironies – to establish library services in the newly independent Republic of the Congo. The caretaker of the apartment, one

James Fair, a former prize-fighter with a flattened nose, lived on the same floor with his charming wife Frances, she of the softest Virginian accent possible. They both took me under their wings. In contrast to Frances's accent, Jimmy spoke from the side of his mouth in a gravelly Chicago tongue that sounded for all the world like an old key being turned in a rusty lock. His memories of his time in the ring were vivid and explicit and he often shuffled around their small kitchen, dodging and feinting as he recalled how he had sorted out So-and-so in the second round. He claimed to know many of the boxing legends of his time, which I took with a large pinch of salt, until I walked into their kitchen one day and there was Gene Tunney, a former world heavyweight champion, sitting there. On another occasion I met the rough and tough little actor James Cagney. They both adored Frances and tolerated Jimmy's boundless exuberance.

I wondered how Lewis would respond to them and, for that matter, they to him. But, in the event, they barely met. In mid-July, Lewis turned up and there began a roller-coaster of a ride for the next four weeks. He had found somewhere nearby to stay, but he came often to my apartment, usually on his way to or from some other encounter.

I learned early on that Lewis was in the process of completing a novel, a play, a volume of short stories, an autobiography and a series of essays on his experiences with his fellow journalists on *Drum* magazine, whom he was to describe many years later as "urbanised, eager, fast-talking and brash" and most of them as heavy drinkers, a description which happened to suit him aptly. He was continuing to write for *Drum* while in the United States, as I was for my newspaper group. The fact that I too was working on a novel paled into insignificance in the face of his outpourings of creativity.

My first, perhaps only, mistake was to introduce Lewis to an attractive young South African émigré whom I was ardently pursuing at the time. He deployed his seduction skills, which he had fine-tuned in Hillbrow, on her and that was the last I saw of them both for at least a week. He turned up alone somewhat shamefacedly and made a half-hearted attempt to apologise but I don't think he was really sorry.

Lewis was the first close black South African friend I had had and it took an encounter in an overseas country to make it happen. He was full of surprises.

On one humid evening, he arrived barefoot on my doorstep and insisted that I join him at a Village nightclub to listen to a fantastic singer he had discovered.

"But, Lewis," I said, "you can't go barefoot."

He laughed uproariously.

"Why not? My feet are black. No one will notice."

He was perfectly right. The singer was stunning and we became regulars, graduating to a front table near the stage where she would acknowledge our arrival with a lovely smile.

I imagined he worked at some stage of the day or night on his wide portfolio of projects but it was difficult to tell, such was his livewire energy in being out and about. However, nothing seemed to be completed. He would dodge my questioning with airy waves of his arms as if to say, "Don't bother me with that now."

I took Lewis to several parties — Saturday evening thrashes that usually ended with 4 a.m. breakfasts in Little Italy before we slept Sunday away — and my friends, mostly *New York Times* journalists, welcomed him as one of the tribe of scribes. But I could see he wasn't particularly comfortable there. The repartee was fast and funny but he didn't quite click. Was it because we were all white? As the party got hotter, Lewis would slip away into the night.

One evening towards the end of his stay, I went with Lewis and my new girlfriend — a sophisticated Japanese actress — to visit friends who lived in a first-floor apartment on the Lower East Side. In those days, the area was something of a poor relation of Greenwich Village, which was starting to become swish. Our friends were among those who had been obliged to move there because they could no longer afford rentals in the Village, and there had been the odd clash between the newcomers and resentful locals.

We had a great evening, and it was 1 a.m. before we left our hosts and made our way downstairs to walk back to the Village. As we turned a corner, we were set upon by a bunch of assailants who had emerged from a club patronised by Puerto Ricans. Our bonhomie dissolved in a flash. It became rapidly clear that our attackers were incensed by a white guy (right) with a white girl (wrong) and a black American (wrong) fraternising together.

The township instincts honed in South Africa surfaced in Lewis. In a flash, he slipped between two parked cars into the safety of the street, calling to us to follow. I remember falling to the sidewalk under the weight of two of the men and crying out fatuous things like "Leave us alone" and "Get off me". There was no doubt that they wanted to teach us a lesson about intruding into their territory as a mixed-race trio. They heaved themselves off me but they were not finished. As I watched in horror, one of them walked up to the Japanese girl and punched her in the eye. Blood spurted out immediately from a cut below her eyebrow. Seemingly satisfied, they disappeared around the corner from which they had come.

Misa was deeply shocked. "My face, my face," she cried, instantly worried about the scar that might result. We took her to the casualty ward of a Village hospital and her wound was stitched.

Next day, the "news" interest surfaced in the two scribes: Lewis and I sent reports back home to our respective publications about the mugging. Mine was given prominent displays. I never saw what Lewis wrote.

As year-end approached, with Lewis long back at Harvard, I remember wishing that I too had left on an exit permit. I did not want to leave New York, leave my girl, leave my wonderful friends, leave my exciting job covering the United Nations and life in the US. I walked down the long tunnel to board my plane home as though I was descending into Purgatory.

Back in South Africa, I heard from Lewis once more. I had been arrested by the Security Police for being in a "Native Reserve" without a permit. It had come about after I had interviewed Chief Albert Luthuli, former president of the African National Congress and Nobel Prize winner, on behalf of *Time* magazine. In terms of a banning order imposed on him, he was permitted to meet one person at a time in a small back office made available to him by an attorney named E.V. Mahomed in the town of Stanger, some fifteen kilometres or so from the Groutville Reserve where he lived.

After he had given me a splendid, off-the-cuff interview which I have always treasured, the chief and I emerged to find it was pouring with rain. I offered him a lift home in my small car. He accepted gratefully. To reach his home, we had to leave the tarred main road to Durban and bounce along a rutted sandy road. When we arrived, he asked me to wait while he went to find his wife to come and greet me. The Security Police got to me first.

"Where's your permit to be in a Native Reserve?"

"I don't have one. It was raining so I gave Chief Luthuli a lift."

I was charged and ordered to appear in the Stanger Magistrate's Court on the following Wednesday.

The incident caused something of a stir and the local *Sunday Times* carried a short front-page report about it. The story was picked up by the agencies and was published in the *New York Times*. Lewis cabled me:

"Congratulations. Way to go."

It was to be forty-six years before I saw him again. Through an intervention by my daughter whose surname Lewis had recognised some years before at a conference in Europe and whom

Lewis had asked whether I was her father, we met at the International Convention Centre in Cape Town in 2007. It was 10 a.m. Lewis was due to participate in a panel discussion at noon. He was into his second beer and he spoke with something of a drawl. I could see it was Lewis alright and he recognised me. The years had descended on us both. I don't know what he made of me, but I searched in vain for any remnants there might be of that wry, bright spirit, full of nervous energy and extraordinary vitality.

I had often wondered in the years following our times together in New York when the work of the budding genius I had identified would take the literary world by storm. Where were the novels, the plays, the short stories he was working on back then, the words that were pouring out of him, that would secure his position among the highest ranks of South African writers? I heard he had left the US soon after the completion of his Harvard stint and made his way to the UK and Europe. He married a British schoolteacher — *hah, finally hooked, eh, Lewis?* — and they had twins. But where were his writings? Did his enforced absence from his homeland dry up his enchanting Muse? What if he had never left?

Someone told me he had entered academia and had obtained a degree from Sussex University which led to professorships in Zambia (quite close to South Africa but not close enough) and at Warsaw University. His focus, it seemed, had turned to the writing of criticism and essays; perhaps they brought in money or were just easier to write than the creative stuff. No doubt there were bouts of drinking, too. I felt infinitely sad.

A debut novel called *Mating Birds* finally appeared in 1986, twenty-five years after we parted. Its theme of love, rape and seduction across the colour line ensured it was banned in South Africa, although somehow I remember securing a copy. To me, it wasn't vintage Nkosi. The spark wasn't there.

When he died in 2010, I was left with a sensation of an unfulfilled promise, a talent that withered. Where did the fault lie? That draconian exit permit? His own frailties, like those of many of the exciting bunch of young writers that *Drum* fostered? The cluster of foreign cultures into which he entered as he wandered the wider world?

Whatever, nothing can erase for me the memory of those magical weeks we spent together in a New York summer.

Crossing the Rubicon

THERE ARE THOSE — ALL OF them aged, or ageing like me — from the editorial segment of the newspaper world who will never forgive me for accepting a transfer, after eight years in their ranks, to the enemy, namely Management. To them, I shall always be a traitor. They supposed I had done it for money: "How could he sell his soul in this despicable way?" In their eyes, and in mine while I was one of them, Management was the antithesis of everything Editorial stood for. It was there to curb editorial initiatives, to pay the staff as little as possible, to control — and cut — costs at every turn and place constant impediments in their way. Above all, Management failed to recognise that the very newspaper existed only because of Editorial and the content it produced.

So why did I do it? Why did I cross the Rubicon? None of my editorial colleagues ever bothered to ask me. This is why.

Until my prized secondment to the New York bureau of the Argus Company for which I worked, my editorial career had progressed well and I loved my job for its variety and unpredictability, for the thrill of finding my story on the front page, for the stimulating company of many (but certainly not all) of my colleagues, for opportunities that presented themselves such as being given at a youthful age the daily and popular "Wayfarer's Page" to write, and then, after three years, being taken on by the London bureau of the company in the heart of Fleet Street. There, for two years, I covered assignments as varied as seconding a South African swimmer in a rowing boat while she attempted to swim the English Channel to living in a tent at an international Scout Jamboree to reporting on Conservative Party and Labour Party conferences. The experience was priceless.

Inevitably, my return to base at *The Daily News* in Durban was somewhat deflating but I felt that at least someone had done some planning in terms of my career development when I was posted to the sub-editors' room. There I learned not only to correct and, if necessary, rewrite copy which came through from the reporters' room where many of my previous colleagues still worked, but also what headlines to post on these stories and then, later, how to lay out pages with a range of different typography. These tasks took me for the first time into the Works Department where the pages were made up in metal and had to be passed by the sub-editor before they were sent to the Machine Room for printing. I learned these things, but the longer I remained in the Subs' Room the more I realised that my forte lay more in the writing than the massaging of material.

So it was with a massive sense of excitement that I took on the one-year secondment to the New York bureau. It proved to be by a distance the best year of my career, and of my life to date. The bureau was based on the fourth floor of the *New York Times* building, just off Broadway in the heart of Manhattan. Within a few weeks I made friends with a group of *Times* staffers who lived, as I did, in Greenwich Village and they welcomed me into their vigorous social lives. My job entailed a certain amount of evening desk work in compiling a daily file from US newspapers to which my company had lifting rights and which was dispatched to South Africa overnight, and so I often came off duty at around 11 p.m., which was when my *New York Times* colleagues did, and we would rollick our way home to Greenwich Village via pubs and pizza houses. But I had the opportunity also of covering the United Nations where the Delegates' Lounge rather than the General Assembly or the Security Council became the source of many of the stories I obtained and dispatched to South Africa in the overnight file.

The year sped by and I left with the heaviest of hearts when my secondment was over and the contract I had signed obliged me to return to my home country.

The crunch came when I walked once more into the newsroom of *The Daily News* in Durban. The same news editor from my first days on the paper came rushing up to me and said: "Jol, I've got just the job for you. I want you to take on the Aquarium beat."

I stared at him in shock and dismay. Did he not have the faintest idea of what I had been doing in New York? Did no one else in Editorial have any idea? Had there not been any planning done on how my growing experience should be utilised other than this insulting suggestion made by the news editor? I asked to see the editor. At some stage in the year I had been away I learned that the previous editor — someone I respected both as a top-rate journalist and as a person — had been promoted to a larger newspaper in the group and had been succeeded by someone who had been editing a small daily in Bloemfontein. My interview with him was extremely discouraging.

For one thing, he seemed to think I had just returned from secondment to the London bureau, not New York, and prattled on about colleagues who worked there that he knew. When I raised the question of career development, he looked uncomfortable as though I was asking him about the price of tea in China. He clearly felt it was not his task to deal with such a subject. After all, he had a newspaper to edit. Disgruntled, I left his office and returned to the newsroom where, for a short period, I busied myself with writing a series of leader-page pieces on my year in New York. I did not embark on the Aquarium beat.

A week later, I came back to the office after reviewing a film for the entertainments page when the news editor once more came rushing up to me with the news that I was to be sent at once as a relief sub-editor to the *Bulawayo Chronicle* in what was then Rhodesia.

This time I demanded to see the manager. His name was Leonard Pickles, whose office was on the top floor of the building. He was known to appear on the editorial floor at 10.30 each morning to have tea with the editor and presumably discuss the fortunes and misfortunes of the newspaper. We knew nothing much about him except that he was a bachelor, had been in the air force in the Second World War and had the usual Management reputation of being tight-fisted. He was rotund

and bald. I can't recall ever having exchanged a
word with him until that time.

I entered his office and found that I had a
daunting walk of some twelve metres or more to
reach his desk behind which he was standing. It
failed to deter me and I am afraid I was extremely
uncouth. My mounting frustrations took the
better of me and I let him have it. The thrust of
my complaint was the complete lack of any career
planning in my case and the cavalier way in which I
had been told, without any form of consultation,
that I was to leave for Bulawayo at short notice as
a relief sub-editor, which was not a direction in
which I wanted to go, either geographically or as
a journalist. To back up my case, I stressed how
much experience I had built up since joining
the paper seven years before, including two
secondments abroad, and how little attention was
being paid to this, as evidenced by the suggestion
that I take on the Aquarium beat. I must say he
took it on the chin. He appeared to be seriously
troubled by what I told him.

"Well, Mr Nuttall, what would you really like
to do?"

I said that I wanted at least to be considered
for the political beat so that I could graduate to
the post of parliamentary correspondent. At this
stage he called in his senior assistant manager,
one John Gittins, and together they discussed

what opportunities might be open to me. It was mooted that I might join the Argus Africa Service, which covered the African continent, but that was ruled out when we realised that my South African passport would be a serious impediment. No immediate alternative opportunity presented itself but, for the first time, I felt that here was a real effort by senior executives — not editorial executives, mind you — to map out a career path for me.

Then suddenly Leonard Pickles leaned forward and said to me,

"Mr Nuttall, would you like to join us in Management?"

It came as a bolt from the blue. Little did I know at the time that there had been a directive from Head Office that required branch managers to upgrade the quality of their line assistants. They should be university graduates and should have had some experience in one or other field of newspaper work. It was interesting to find later that accounting experience — in my vocabulary, number crunching — was not specified.

Mr Pickles caught me by surprise, both by his unexpected offer and by what appeared to be his genuine concern over my distress. I have to confess that, equally unexpectedly and contrary to all my preconceptions, I rather liked him and I calmed down. It was agreed that I would think about his offer and, in the meantime, I would take on the Bulawayo assignment. It certainly seemed more interesting than anything else on offer — and so it proved, even when my stay was extended by a further six weeks.

While I was in Rhodesia, with time to think things through at a distance, including the possibility that I was contemplating marriage, I wrote to Len Pickles, accepting his offer to join his staff. I received a warm reply in which he expressed his delight at my decision.

It was to start a rich twenty-five-year career in Management during which my eyes were opened to all the other dimensions that make up what a newspaper is, and I was to rise from a lowly assistant in the manager's office of the Durban branch to all but the highest position in the group, as general manager of *The Star* and the *Sowetan* and a director of the company. I also filled numerous newspaper industry positions, most notably for two years as president of the Newspaper Press Union (NPU) and chairman of the Audit Bureau of Circulations.

It was all a long way from that Aquarium beat. But I was never to forget my editorial origins. And when I took early retirement at the age of fifty-seven, the managing director described me in his farewell speech as "an editor's manager". I took it as the best compliment I could have wished for.

Greyton Passeggiata

THE PASSEGGIATA AS IT IS practised in Europe — in Italy, for example — is a slow, dignified affair. It takes place as the light begins to fade. The participants are prosperous, elderly couples, formally dressed — he in a suit and black shoes, she in a tailored skirt and comfortable brogues. They both wear hats. Her right hand is tucked under his left elbow as they walk. The object is to be seen for who and what they are: a couple who have made a success of their lives, their marriage, their bank balances, who belong in their level of society in which they see themselves as pillars.

They promenade sedately along the same route they have used for years. To some of those they meet — other couples participating in the same ritual — they nod politely and he raises his hat an inch above his head, signalling that their own station in life is a notch or two above that of those they are passing. To others, they stop and shake hands or even give little embraces, with perhaps a peck on an extended cheek, and there is an exchange of small talk. Not for too long because there are more nods and hands to be shaken before they reach the end of their designated route and turn for home as the shadows lengthen.

In Greyton, the Cape country village where I have a cottage, it's different. The passeggiata is a riotous affair, full of overtones of noise and bravado and undertones of sexual conquest. It's at its best on a Friday.

As in Europe, it takes place in late light. It is payday. Daar is geld in die sak en petrol in die tjorrie. The shops are closing and the young girls who work in them are making their way home along the main street. I watch them from the open stoep of the local inn that has been there forever. I have come for a beer or two after digging and planting and reaping.

Suddenly, from the end of the village towards which the girls are heading comes the roar of revved-up engines. In seconds, the street is transformed. The young laaities come racing along, hooters blaring, brakes squealing as they spot a maiden they desire. The passengers are leaning so far out of the cars' windows that they practically fall out. Their hands reach for the girls, who have stopped to watch the procession, giggling and covering their ears as the shouts grow wilder and more suggestive.

The cars race along the street and then turn and come streaking back. Their occupants spot me, and others, on the stoep and, for a few moments, they turn their attention to us. The insults, delivered in choice country Afrikaans, fly up at us and they give us one-finger, two-finger signals of disdain at our uppity vantage point.

Then it is time to close in on their prey. They screech to a halt and open their doors. Some of the girls step in. There are shouts and screams. The hotrod engines rev to new pitches of noise and, in an instant, they are gone.

The Greyton promenade is over. They have given the village back to those of us on the stoep. We return to our beers and glasses of wine. The quiet descends and the night closes in.

On Managing Stress

I HAVE BEEN INTRIGUED TO discover that my faithful *Oxford Concise Dictionary* not only defines the word "stress" as, among other things, "demand upon physical or mental energy" but goes on to list it as a *disease* suffered by "managers etc. subjected to continual stress".

So *that* was what was wrong with me all those years ago when I all but fainted at a board meeting of the South African Press Association! I had a disease.

I do remember there was awful panic among the other members as I excused myself from the board table and stumbled into an armchair, my head spinning and a frightening sensation invading me that I might be having a dreaded heart attack, or something.

"Loosen his tie," one of them said.

"Give him some tea with sugar," said another.

"Phone for a car to take him home," a third suggested, no doubt anxious to return to the agenda.

The news spread quickly because that evening I even had a call from the chairman, enquiring about my health or, should I say, my disease.

The following day I went to see my GP, who checked me over and then gave me a withering look.

"You seem to think you are Superman," he said. And then, to his great credit, he told me to start my imminent year-end leave immediately. I felt better at once.

Of course, the GP was right. As I ascended the ladder of seniority, the ever more frenetic my working life had become. I rushed from one industry meeting to another while squeezing into intervals during the day and often at weekends the demands of my job as general manager of *The Star*.

It was clearly a "wake-up" call. So, what to do about it? This is a dilemma, of course, that has faced multitudes of those in authority since time immemorial, but let's dwell on the present age. How do those in pressured jobs handle stress? A first step, I suppose, is to recognise the symptoms when stress is encroaching, but even cleverer is to avoid the likelihood of the disease — there's that word again – launching its attack. People run, and cycle, and pound the machines in gyms, and cut out smoking, and cut down on drinking, all in the hope of doing this. A healthy *lifestyle* is the thinking.

I left all this a little late but, during my extended period of leave and knowing I needed to take action because I was not Superman after all, I came up with various possible solutions. I decided I must step down from some of the lesser bodies and committees on which I served, win back some time and manage it more efficiently. What was it they said on that course I attended? Choose the five most important things to do each day and make sure they are done. Write them down on a pad and tick them off as you complete them. Delegate more, of course. Why otherwise have two assistant managers, both angling for your job anyway? Work from home more, where people can't interrupt you. Remember how well it worked when you were convalescing from that burst appendix and your heads of department had to come to see you there. You successfully attacked that economic downturn in no time.

I tried all of these steps on my return from leave. They did make a difference and the symptoms of the disease receded. But something was still missing, something that would make me switch off before and after my working day, some kind of therapy. It was then that I remembered the hens ...

When I was a boy, my twin brother and I, living on two acres, began assembling a menagerie. We started with a pair of pigeons, which rapidly became a squad of pigeons, and then two ducks, before acquiring six plump Rhode Island Red hens from the local police sergeant's wife. Each day we collected their eggs and took them in a little basket into the kitchen and my mother was delighted.

Why not, I thought, try it again?

Behind our property on the Parktown Ridge in Johannesburg was a series of terraces, each backed by stone walling. On one of them I had established a vegetable garden in furtherance of my suppressed desire to be a small-time farmer. It seemed logical to construct a chicken run adjacent to it. A brick-laying course I had done came in useful for the surrounding base into which I sank wire netting so it was predator-proof, followed by thatched roofing and a gate to provide access. I recalled that hens do not sleep on Mother Earth at night but on perches, so these too were installed, as were nesting boxes.

The first occupants were acquired from a small-holding near Pretoria. They travelled back to Parktown in the boot of my car. They seemed undeterred by the darkness. I found that one of them had laid an egg en route, which seemed a good omen.

And so it proved. Each morning before I left for work, I paid a visit to my hens to feed and water them, and each late afternoon I let them out of the run to extend their horizons and closed a hand around the eggs that were in the nesting boxes. As I did so, the cares and strains of office melted away and I became a saner and pleasanter member of the household.

Just as in Management, however, it was not long before a challenge arose which required a creative solution. As they were of good breeding, unlike battery hens, the maternal instinct overtook my lot from time to time. The problem was that, sans rooster, their eggs were not fertile. The hens were not to know that, and sat on and on in anticipation of the eggs hatching. I learned to my horror that the instinct was so strong that, albeit starving and dehydrated, this would continue until death would us part.

The solution was ingenious and heart-warming. I was advised to buy a few day-old chicks from a local pet shop and, at the dead of night, insert them under the broody hen. Late one evening, I crept up to the run and did what I had been told. It worked like magic. Soft maternal noises immediately emanated from the mother hen, because that is what she became, as she tucked her brood under her. The following morning, there she was, fussing and calling and scratching around the run, with the chicks scurrying after her. And so I bred for succession.

It was only as the chicks blossomed into maturity that I realised that one of them was becoming larger than the rest and, furthermore, was developing plumed tail feathers and a handsome comb. A magnificent rooster, fed on the finest of poultry foods, supplemented by greens from my vegetable garden, became a significant presence in the run. With six hens to meet his voracious needs and to reserve the best perch for him on which to roost at night, he clearly thought he was in paradise.

So proud of his lordly domain was he, however, that it led to his departure. The silly fellow took to beating the dawn by crowing repeatedly from some ungodly hour as if to challenge any other roosters in Parktown to match his bounty. Our godly neighbour, a dominee who needed an undisturbed night's sleep in order to fulfil his duties to his flock, lodged a firm complaint. One man's loss proved to be another man's gain: our gardener took the rooster off to his rural home where, I gathered, he reigned supreme for many years and no doubt enriched the quality of the poultry stock in the region.

If there is one major similarity between the

hierarchy of the business world and that in the chicken run, it is to be found in what is known as the pecking order. Take tea sets as they existed in one of South Africa's top companies for many years. They defined the particular rank of individuals in the management structure. Those at entry level were brought their tea in plain cups and saucers on tin trays but, if they were fortunate enough to advance up the ladder, the quality steadily improved until one day, lo and behold, a silver tray with a silver tea set and bone china cups and saucers became the order of the day.

With hens, the pecking order is a fundamental feature of their lives. The strongest and the fittest reign. It manifests itself essentially when it comes to settling on a perch for the night. The lesser mortals hop on the perches first, choosing the best spots and thereby hoping to establish that occupation is nine-tenths of the law. But they are steadily and rudely shoved aside as the night advances until the weakest end up at the very end of the perch or, if necessary, kicked off it altogether. During the day they are pecked unmercifully if they intrude on the space of a hen higher up the order and are chased around the run.

Socialists would argue that the solution is an enlarged scratch patch during the day, where there is space for all and plenty of exactly similar perching rods for the night. Perhaps this would mitigate the humiliation of the weak, but the idiots persist in trying to move up the ranks.

It's the same the whole world over.

Note: I cannot be sure of the exact extent to which the keeping of hens ameliorated my levels of stress, but they must have helped because I never suffered from the *disease* again.

The Sinister Eighties

IT IS NOT POSSIBLE TO HAVE LIVED in South Africa in the 1980s as general manager of the country's highest-selling daily newspapers — *The Star* and, for some of the decade, the *Sowetan* — without trying to convey some sense of the tensions and tribulations, and of certain triumphs, that went with it.

In 1981, at the age of forty-seven, I was posted unexpectedly from Durban, where I was managing the Argus Company's cluster of newspapers, to head the company's flagship, *The Star*, in Johannesburg because the incumbent had decided to emigrate to Australia. Although my wife and I were both born and raised in Natal, as it was then known, we were delighted to return to the highveld where we had spent eleven years previously and where nobody asked you where you went to school or what your father did. You were your own person, and you made it or you didn't on your own abilities.

I knew from the seven years I had spent as senior assistant manager of *The Star* from 1968 to 1975 that it was rather like a battleship that required immense effort to change its course if that was the purpose. After all, it had been around on the very same site, on the corner of President and Sauer streets — opposite where the ANC's Luthuli House is today — since 1887, just one year after gold was discovered in the mining camp that became South Africa's largest city.

The Star had long been an institution in the city and the wider region and had built up a loyal and mostly devoted readership, chiefly — but not only — among whites. Because of this, it had attracted a substantial share of the advertising market, so it was a very profitable entity, not to be tampered with idly by an ambitious new manager or his partner, the editor. The two were jointly responsible for the well-being of *The Star* and were required by the board to work closely together.

However, *The Star* at that time had acquired a reputation among those who supported it, both readers and advertisers, as being somewhat stuck in its ways. Hence its nickname, Aunty Argus.

What is more, although its sales were easily the highest of all daily newspapers in the country, they consistently failed to break through the two hundred thousand barrier, try as successive general managers and editors might to achieve this. Each time the magic figure appeared to be within *The Star*'s grasp, an unavoidable increase in the price at which the newspaper was sold resulted in a despairing retreat.

Clearly, the first objective I set myself, in collaboration with the editor, was to pierce the barrier and to go on from there to dispel the Aunty Argus image. To help us do so, we redesigned the structure of the newspaper into what we called the five-point Star: a five-section paper that included a split main body, the better to accommodate the high volume of supermarket advertising on offer as well as provide more editorial columns, a substantial classified section of eighteen pages or more, a tabloid called *Tonight!* to cover the entertainment scene and a second tabloid called *Today* which focused on lifestyle. In its new shape, *The Star* became the most beautiful newspaper I had ever worked on.

It took us the first few years of my ten-year tenure to crack the two hundred thousand barrier but we did it, in part by following a world-wide trend among afternoon newspapers towards moving distribution in further-flung areas to the morning. Availability became the key.

I threw a party — known in the newspaper world as a wetstone — for all one thousand staffers when we cleared two hundred thousand for the first time, and the hallelujahs rang loud and clear. As news values escalated later in the decade, we hit 247,305 average sales a day — and I have a T-shirt to this day to prove it.

Those were the triumphs. But they took place against a continually darkening political landscape as the pillars of apartheid began to crumble and the Nationalist government became ever more fevered in its attempts to shore up the edifice it had created over nearly forty years. Newspapers were prime targets and the government would have dearly loved to close the lot of us, in particular what it singled out as "die gevaarlike Engelse pers". Instead, although it was always twitching to act, it imposed ever more severe restrictions on what newspapers could print and what they could not, whom they could quote and whom they could not (an ever-growing list of banned people). Editing a newspaper became what was described as walking blindfold through a minefield. A team of media lawyers was on constant call to guide our editorial staff on what the multiple laws permitted us to publish. Our instruction to the lawyers in giving us this advice was to allow us to walk as close to the edge of the precipice as possible without falling off.

In addition to multiple responsibilities within the Argus Company, management was required to serve on the numerous organisations which existed to further the interests of the media industry as a whole. These responsibilities had to be absorbed into an executive's portfolio as part of the workload. I found myself being drafted onto committees of various kinds. During my time as general manager, Johannesburg, and a board member of the newspaper company, I served for two years as chairman of the Audit Bureau of Circulations, which issued the all-important average circulations of its members to the industry. The country's advertisers based major decisions on where to place their custom in the light of these averages, often coupled with the number of readers per copy a newspaper attracted, so the veracity of these figures was critical.

The most senior of all the print organisations was the Newspaper Press Union, known by all as the NPU. The name was a misnomer in the sense that it was certainly not a trade union but, instead, an employer body that dealt with a lengthy agenda of matters relevant to the printed word. In that sense, it was a kind of newspaper chamber of commerce on which all the major companies, both Afrikaans- and English-speaking, were represented. They took turns in nominating members to serve for two years as president, each of whom undertook a sort of apprenticeship for two years as vice-president to learn the ropes. After years as a member of the NPU, which gave me a wide grounding on a number of major issues, I was elected as vice-president and then, in the last years of the eighties, as president. It was in those years that I was frequently confronted by the full brunt of the apartheid machine. A sinister and deeply uncomfortable time it became, one which has left me questioning deeply in the decades since whether the actions and initiatives we took in good faith stand up to scrutiny.

The strategy of the state was to prevent the publication of as much as they could of their repressive and brutal actions against their opponents within the borders of South Africa and in their cross-border intrusions and ensuing atrocities in southern Africa and at times further afield. At all costs, no information was to be released on deaths in detention and on the loss of life among South African forces in the field. The sons of our readers were dying in police hands or being killed in combat in Angola and Namibia, and their parents were being informed, but newspapers were not permitted to confirm this in print.

Our strategy during my tenure became to extract, through direct negotiation with government, as much information as we could in order to fulfil our commitment to readers to "tell it like it is", to borrow *The Star*'s slogan which the newspaper had adopted in those times. I had become a strong believer in the merits of negotiation rather than direct confrontation in two other areas of my industry work: the first was in the vital field of newsprint supply and the second in negotiations with trade unions over wage increases.

After importing newsprint for years, South Africa had become self-sufficient in supply through the establishment first of Sappi and then of Mondi. As an incentive to the two companies, Gencor and Anglo American, which built the mills and planted or acquired the huge acreages of timber necessary to produce newsprint, the government had permitted them to charge newspaper companies the same for their newsprint as had been paid for imported newsprint, even though the cost was substantially less. Successive NPU presidents had attempted without success to secure a contract with the mills that would overcome the arbitrary increases that were being imposed, based on overseas newsprint prices. With my colleagues on the NPU's newsprint committee, I opened negotiations with the mills on a basis similar to that I had developed in negotiating with editorial and printers' unions over salary and wage increases. Essentially, they began with both parties declaring their opening positions and then negotiating, and caucusing, and renegotiating, and recaucusing, until, at a critical moment, the two positions were close enough for a final mandate to seal an agreement. It worked, and we walked away with a newsprint contract.

I intended to adopt the same strategy in negotiating with government over the release of more information to NPU member newspapers. The two critical areas of focus were the departments of defence and of police. My predecessors had established liaison committees, on which NPU members and members of the conference of editors were nominated to serve, and meetings with agendas were held with senior officials of the sections, usually in Pretoria. On occasion, ministers attended. The approach was to secure agreement that journalists from NPU newspapers, both Afrikaans- and English-language, should be granted accreditation by both departments, which would entitle them to be given for publication what had hitherto been regarded as classified information.

On my nomination to serve on these committees, which I accepted with great reluctance, it quickly became apparent to me that what was happening was the use of confidential background briefings to our members on the strict condition that nothing was to be printed. In other words, the departments were trying to open our eyes to the severity of the challenges they were facing, both internally and externally, so that we would understand why it was not in the public interest that this should be made known, in order to prevent panic and alarm spreading through what was essentially the white populace. There were those on the committees on our side who bought into this line, which made the task of the rest of us more difficult.

I was soon to learn, when I was required to lead our delegation, that the negotiating techniques I had deployed successfully elsewhere were to fall on barren ground. At the encounters themselves, an insufferable air of affability, as tea and sandwiches were served, tended to develop among members from both sides in the full knowledge that, once the talks began, intransigence would reign.

The full horror broke when an invitation was extended to our members of the police committee to attend the next meeting at Parliament in Cape Town as the minister, Adriaan Vlok, wished to be present. We knew Vlok as an outwardly obsequious man, anxious to be loved and understood, but in actual fact deep into implementing the full panoply of vicious repression that the laws encouraged. I believe now that we should have declined the invitation but, ever in the hope that we might win the concessions we sought, we went. Sure enough, the minister was present and chaired the meeting, which brought little cheer. What was to follow was worse: he extended a warm invitation to us to attend a luncheon he had arranged in a private dining room in the House. The atmosphere was awkward, to say the least, but the minister was undaunted. He rose to his feet and spoke about the importance of close understanding between his department and the media, and about what a difficult job he and his colleagues had to perform in the interests of the country.

Then he moved around the table and presented each of our members with a small gift. I was sitting next to Joe Latakgomo, previously editor of the *Sowetan* and now an assistant editor of *The Star*. We opened the gifts and were gobsmacked to find inside a pair of police emblazoned cufflinks. He and I left the meeting together.

"What shall we do with these?" I remember Joe asking me. Just ahead of us was a municipal drain.

"How about there, Joe?"

Without a moment's hesitation, we flung them down the drain, and walked on, feeling just a tiny touch better.

❧

There were those who said the NPU should not

have participated in those liaison committees with government and should not have undertaken to establish – under dire threats by Prime Minister B.J. Vorster and his successors to implement direct state censorship – a Press Council, chaired by a judge, to monitor complaints about editorial coverage brought before it by politicians or members of the public and to discipline those found to have transgressed a press code. Instead, they said, the NPU should have called the government's bluff.

In his major work, *Editors under Fire*, former editor of *The Star* Harvey Tyson writes:

"The battle of an authoritarian regime against an independent press became, over the years, a game of chess in which both sides knew most of the gambits ... Each side was too wary to try all in a single blow. Of course there were Cabinet ministers who wished blatantly to take control of the press, but they were restrained by their colleagues and by forces within the party and the party press. Of course there were newspaper people who sought the grand gesture which would end in the newspapers and themselves dying as heroes and martyrs. But they too were restrained by their peers."

It is worth recording that, of the four major companies that belonged to the NPU, two were Afrikaans-language groups that actively supported the government's apartheid policies. Agreement to ignore the belligerent threats to impose state censorship could not have been obtained.

In my mouth the distaste remains. The interactions that took place were personally repugnant, the subject matter underscored repeatedly by apartheid's atrocities. The only ultimate satisfaction to be drawn from the saga was the collapse of the regime while the press survived to tell the story of the birth of a new South Africa. It brought me a modicum of comfort in its aftermath.

Lunch at the Blaasbalk

OBSERVED FROM THE NATIONAL road from Cape Town to Port Elizabeth, the small town of Botrivier at the foot of Houw Hoek Pass, is – to use an Afrikaans expression – botstil. In other words, very quiet. You might even say it is tjoepstil, that is: ever so quiet.

But drive in on a Friday lunchtime, past the weekend townhouses, all painted white and mostly closed up, to the middedorp and you will discover the stamp of the local farming community: the wheat growers, the sheep farmers, the wine and olive buffs. Their paraphernalia is everywhere: the trucks, the pallets, the boxes, the sacks of fertiliser, a tractor or two brought in to be repaired. Prominent in the central square is the liquor outlet and the shop-trying-to-be-a-supermarket.

And the local hotel.

Because it is Friday and it's lunchtime, the customers in their khakis and weather-stained hats are seated on the verandah. Their Jack Russells are sitting on their laps and they are into the beers. It's what all that hard work during the week was for.

While I wait for a friend from Hermanus to join me, I wander the square and then the grounds of the hotel. They belong to a previous era, in feel, in shape, in architecture. They project a sense of hanging on by their fingertips. Inside, the hotel is cavernous. I follow long passages in dark spaces and then I emerge on what I recognise as a dance floor. A sign says "Die/The Blaasbalk Restaurant". I wonder at the meaning of blaasbalk. There is a huge fireplace in a corner. Is that a clue?

In a moment, I am lost in a haze of imagining the dances in village halls, tiekiedraai and langarm and pump-handle swoops and swirls. How many exact occasions like these have taken place in the Blaasbalk, how many hearts have been won and hopes dashed?

We lunch on the verandah. Along the way, the second beers have been sunk and the third summoned. There is a smartly dressed waiter and a menu. Basically, though, it's lamb tjops or steak, with chips. My friend orders the tjops and I ask for the steak, medium rare. The waiter stares at me. Then he writes in his order book. I wish I could see what he writes.

How would we like our chips? Slap or crispy? That's a new one. Wow! "Slap," says my friend, "crispy," say I. We ask for wine. He winces. But a bottle of red comes.

My steak arrives. It is just on the right side of well-done. The chips are perfect, each to his own. The wine takes hold and our conversation dives into the realms of recollection and hilarity. At that point, for a little while, there is nowhere else I would rather be.

Note: Blaasbalk is the Afrikaans word for "bellows". Hence the link between the name and the fireplace.

Remembrance

THE HUMAN MIND HAS AN endless capacity to skip from one thought to another, particularly when its owner is indulging in what Marcel Proust called à la recherche du temps perdu — remembrance of things past — and William Wordsworth summarised as recollections in tranquillity. As evidence of this, I find that often, when I think about flyfishing, a lifetime passion of mine, my recollections turn to one specific day on a specific river in a specific place ...

I am hacking up Naude's Nek, the highest commercial pass in South Africa (meaning that two-wheel-drive vehicles can traverse it, with a wing and a prayer), in the company of a flyfishing master in the making named Fred Steynberg. We are in his 4x4, which has a bumper sticker which reads *All roads lead to Rhodes*. At last, that has applied to my road too. Ahead of us is a day's fishing on the upper reaches of the Bell River.

At eight thousand feet, just four hundred shy of the summit, we turn off the road and make our way down towards the crystal-clear runs below us.

Fred tells me that he spends most, if not all, of every day of the season fishing. Over the past two or three years, he has converted totally to upstream fishing, with dry fly, emerger or nymph. In particular, nymphing — using a double-header with strike indicator — fascinates him. On a good night he can tie thirty nymph patterns.

"Look," I say to this thirty-one-year-old veteran of eighteen seasons, "I don't expect to catch fish on my first day on a river I've never fished before."

He gives me a withering look and says, "Follow me, Oom Jolyon," as he plunges along the riverbank. "There's a two-pounder, do you see it? And there's another, right next to it, just below that ledge."

Fred has those X-ray eyes of a countryman that see deep into pools and runs, spotting fish long before the ordinary mortal can. But, as we make our way to the spot he has selected for us to begin, I start to see fish too. Dozens of them. I realise the river is alive with trout and I find myself itching with anticipation.

We reach a dream of a pool: strong fall at the head flowing into a deep, dark cup before smoothing out over ledges running the length of each bank. I'm dying to start fishing, but Fred won't be rushed. "Have a cold drink," he says, digging into his rucksack as we crouch at the foot of the pool. "The fish may have seen us as we moved down the bank. Give them time to settle."

Finally he moves into position well back from the edge of the bank and peers into the pool. "Hey, there's a four-pounder just beyond the left-hand ledge there and at least two other big ones. Go for it."

For a moment I have stage fright: I'll never be able to do it. Then I call on my own thirty years of experience on rivers and move as quietly as I can into the lower lip of the pool and draw out some line. The tiny RAB dry fly bounces on the palm of my hand. Silently, I offer up a prayer to the river gods: Please don't let me fluff this one.

The line goes out straight and true, and the fly lands like thistledown on the water.

"Good," Fred whispers, "but you need to be three feet further up. The fish are under the ledge."

The tension all curled up inside me, I cast again, and the gods stay on my side. The fly bobs slowly back towards me on the gentle current.

"There he comes ... he's coming ... he's taken it."

I strike and the barbless Number 14 fly hits home as the trout rises, sucks in the fly and turns. The weight of the fish is evident immediately as it dives into the deep water below the fall and I know there's a long, hard road ahead for both of us. Already, though, there's a thrill in me: I have hooked my trout, copybook-style.

Fred is delighted. He bounces along the bank, watching the cut and thrust of the struggle between man and fish. "Dit is 'n meneer, 'n regte meneer," he shouts.

We time the fight. Five minutes pass in a flash, then it's ten. The fish shows no sign of tiring. Fred has spotted it several times from his vantage point on the bank — "it's a cock fish, I can see the spawning colours along its sides" — but, knee-deep in the river, I know the trout only by the feel of it. At fifteen minutes I apply pressure for the first time and turn the fish's head for a moment, but this serves only to invigorate it further. I realise anew how the use of lightweight tackle evens the battle. Nevertheless, the strength of the trout astounds me.

At nineteen minutes, patience and pressure win through and I bring my beauty to Fred's net. He lies there, suddenly supine, the lower jaw of his great head jutting upwards. I cannot get over the kaleidoscope of colours on his sides. We take his length and we estimate his weight at three pounds something: my biggest river fish by some distance. Fred produces a camera from somewhere within his rucksack. It's a great moment, but I am anxious to release the rainbow, to set him free so he can recover from the epic struggle. The tiny hook slips easily from his upper jaw and I hold him upright in the current for a few seconds. Then he glides off upstream and dips under the ledge from where I first rose him. I feel myself go limp.

"So," says Fred, "you reckon you don't catch fish on your first day out on a new river. Remember, Oom Jolyon, this is not any old river. This is the Bell."

Rabbit Comes for Christmas

THERE HAS BEEN A LONG tradition in our family that, wherever its members may be in the world, they should gather for Christmas. They come like swallows to the same nesting place, year after year. Most of them arrive pale and wan after the exertions of their professional and domestic lives but, in no time, they perk up as good food and rest flow into their veins. New arrivals have no choice other than to come along with their parents but somehow, as they grow older, the spirit of the season, coupled with the embrace of the family, rapidly absorbs them into the tradition.

The same applies to family pets. Benjy, the golden cocker spaniel, attended sixteen

Christmases before being denied a seventeenth by a fatal bout of biliary. A bouncy fellow by the name of Hugo was accorded membership status recently and looks set to extend it for some years to come. So it was only natural that the youngest granddaughter's pet rabbit should become the latest addition to the list.

However, the logistics of arranging for Rabbit to join the annual gathering proved more complex than, for example, those that applied to Benjy, who simply jumped into the car and settled contentedly in his basket for the journey from Johannesburg to the coast. It became apparent that Rabbit would have to fly, along with the rest of his family.

I was deputed to explore the details with the chosen airline. I dialled the number and, after asking for Domestic Bookings, found that I should call the cargo division instead. I hadn't pictured Rabbit as cargo but I duly did so and the following conversation ensued:

"Good morning. Could you tell me, please, what's involved in flying a pet from Johannesburg to Cape Town."

"Morning. If you give me the flight details, I'll make a booking for you right away."

"Eh, at this stage I'm just checking on what's involved."

"Oh. Well, you have to supply a container for

your pet and bring it to the cargo section two hours before your flight. You pay according to the weight and volume of the container."

So far, so remarkably good.

She went on:

"What we recommend is that your dog should be given a tranquilliser ..."

"Excuse me, it's not a dog."

"Well, your cat then."

I began to be overcome with mirth.

"Actually, it's — eh — a rabbit."

"A rabbit? Going on holiday?"

"Oh, yes," I said, "rabbits need a holiday like everyone else."

"Really?"

We both became convulsed with laughter. I couldn't resist a follow-up.

"Look," I said, "wouldn't it simplify things if the rabbit travelled in the passenger section with my granddaughter?"

It may have been something to do with the silly season but she replied airily:

"Oh, sure. Why not!"

"Does that mean", I asked, "that Rabbit would have to go through the X-ray machine?"

Mutual hysteria ended the conversation, but I got her drift.

The next step was to seek not only to replicate at my Kommetjie property in Cape Town the lifestyle to which Rabbit was accustomed at his Johannesburg home and garden, sleeping under my granddaughter's bed, but to ensure that he was protected from predators such as passing dogs, my neighbours' large ginger cat and raptors that fly overhead in search of a tasty meal. I put out the word and soon there came a response that held out promise of a solution.

I received information that there was a rabbit rights activist who was involved in rescuing homeless rabbits from unhappy endings and generally tending to their needs. But I was warned:

"Beware. For all we know, she might be a rabid rights activist who does all sorts of nefarious things in the name of saving rabbits."

Henceforth, this unknown person became known as the RRRA. I phoned her in trepidation. A charming voice answered. One minute of conversation and I knew I was on to a gem. Not only did the RRRA assure me that rabbits were good travellers, which was comforting to know, but she offered me a large rabbit hutch which her rescue operation could lend me for the Christmas season as a base for Rabbit until he had become used to his new habitat.

That was not all. This fountain of knowledge on the subject of rabbits advised me to acquire the smallest cat collar I could find, and a harness and lead to go with it, so that Rabbit could be taken safely on walks. My mind swam with a vision of him hopping along the Kommetjie boardwalk as all and sundry gave way to this unique sight. But where to acquire such equipment?

"There's a vet shop", said the RRRA, "just near the place where you have to collect the hutch. Ask them."

Is it possible that the modern world produces such Samaritans?

The vet shop not only obliged with all the basic requirements for Rabbit's seaside home, such as pet bedding, a bag of lucerne which Rabbit could munch, and a packet of pellets, but we were also shown an astonishing range of harness and lead sets. We were advised to abandon the idea of a collar. My granddaughter chose a beautifully made, brightly coloured set that had the added advantage of glowing in the dark.

The stage was now equipped with all the props.

Rabbit flew. Rabbit arrived in Cape Town and was collected at the airport's Pet Lounge. He was crouching in his small container with his long ears laid back and his nose twitching fifty to the dozen. Understandably, he looked rather forlorn. But it took only a few minutes of my granddaughter's loving care to restore his confidence.

Rabbit had a great holiday with other members of the clan although he flatly refused to don the harness. This seemed a pity, but it looks lovely, hanging with the lead in my entrance hall, next to the walking sticks, and glowing in the dark. Perhaps Rabbit will change his mind when he comes again next year.

My Life

I N YEARS I AGE
As time flows.
Despite my rage
The tally grows.

Of my allotted span
I'm left with only five
To use as best I can,
To sink or thrive.

That's what the books teach.
Well — we shall see
If what they preach
Applies to me.

For one, they cannot kill
The boy within me still
Who sees his life ahead
As something far from dead.

They cannot take away
A sense of more to come,
The feeling that each day
Compounds life's sum.

There's still so much to do,
To love, to feel, to give,
To dream, and wonder who
Bestows the right to live.

My life is my life
Given to me to fill.
Grant me time to do that,
Then I'll be still.

On Being a
Grandfather

THE BIRTH OF MY FIRST grandchild seemed to me to be such a determinant of advancing age that I flatly refused to be known by any of the usual versions of that status: Grandpa, Granddad, Gramps, Pop or Dobbs — as a friend of mine ended up being called.

"I would like her to call me Jolyon," I declared.

That, I thought, should put a stop to any of the above titles or other far more humiliating labels that might emerge from the mouths of babes. What's more, whatever old ladies might tut-tut about, it would show us to be a progressive, modern-day family free of the bonds of tradition.

And so it was with Grandchildren One, Two,

Three and Four, two each from my son and my daughter. Although my name is not easy to pronounce, they all took to it unto the manner born. Recently, I asked Granddaughter One, now an intelligent eighteen, whether it had ever seemed odd to her that she should call me by my first name rather than addressing me as, say, Granddad.

"Never thought about it," she said and returned to checking messages on her smartphone.

I have found that children are like that. They talk to the point. They don't beat about the bush. They say what they think. Their minds are not cluttered – yet – by social mores that define what you can do and say, and what you can't. There is so much to learn from them. It has been an unexpected discovery that has come simply from interacting with my grandchildren. No wonder Wordsworth declared that the Child is Father of the Man. Finally, I have come to understand what he meant.

All four differ from one another, in their personalities, their interests, their likes and dislikes, their natures. I have to adjust, depending on which one I am with. One enjoys being teased and laughs along with it, another hates it. Two – one from each family – are passionate about the outdoors and climbing trees and onto roofs and exploring their environment. The other two occupy themselves less energetically in more cerebral things. All four are voracious readers.

There was a lengthy gap between the arrival of the first-born and the other three, who appeared in rapid succession. This meant that First-Born enjoyed an exclusive focus for five years, a privilege she was forced to give up with, I suspect, some reluctance. Her family all danced attendance around her and she verged on the edge at times of becoming a little prima donna. I was in the middle of a rare round of golf with my son when his wife phoned with the ecstatic news that Alice had produced her first tooth. Hurrahs all round. There were to be many other "firsts", first birthday party, first steps, first words, first time she had eaten a worm, first day at pre-school. They continue to this day: first time up on points as a developing ballet dancer.

Grandchildren seem to have the gift of bringing fresh life, and fresh familial love, into the hearts and minds of their parents' parents. My father, a classicist, anointed his five grandchildren with Latin titles: Nuttall Minimus Primus, Nuttall Minima Secunda, Nuttall Minimus Tertius, Nuttall Minima Quarta and, to hoots of laughter, Nuttall Minimus Quintus.

In later years, he wrote a priceless sketch of family history called *Tales of Another Grandfather*, which he typed out laboriously on an ancient typewriter and of which he provided each child with a copy in a bound folder. He did what every grandparent should do in some form or another: capture for subsequent generations what is otherwise lost forever. He recounted what he knew, warts and all, without attempting to put a gloss on it.

I have travelled three times to the United States with my two youngest grandchildren and their parents, who had teaching and research commitments on two Ivy League campuses, and once with them all to Italy. A certain amount of child-minding was included and even a little tutoring, which I didn't mind one bit, in return for having time to explore the environments in which I found myself. Under the watchful eye of their parents, they adapted to these places with almost effortless ease and absorbed their experiences into their development.

They all loved my wife Jean, who had opted to be called Nonna, drawn from her passion for all things Italian. She bonded with each of them in a special way, most obviously because she never talked down to them and also because she was fun. Games of cards became hilarious episodes as allegations of cheating and indignant denial rang out when someone won. She used to run competitions by seeing who could jump the furthest from a ramp down onto the lawn below, measuring each jump with a leaf. We had a cherry guava tree which became known as the Shaking Tree when it was laden with fruit. I would shake the tree and the children present would see who could collect the most little red guavas in their baskets, with a prize for the winner.

When Jean died, Alice was twelve, Zoë was seven, Léa was six and Aniel was four. Each was devastated in her or his own way but their comprehension of what had happened to her varied. We held a private family cremation service in the little Italianate chapel attached to the Priory of the Catholic Church in Kommetjie, and all four grandchildren attended with their parents. The coffin was wheeled into the chapel just before the service began. It was an occasion when once again the directness of young children emerged strongly. They sat quietly during the actual service, the three youngest, not accustomed to being in a church or chapel, seemingly bewildered. But after the family pall-bearers had taken the coffin out to the waiting hearse and it had driven away, the questions began. In their simplicity, they were among the hardest I have ever had to answer.

"What was in that box?" Aniel wanted to know. It was obvious that he had no idea that it was his Nonna. I explained as gently as I could, but he was clearly nonplussed.

Then Léa asked, "But where are they taking Nonna?" As I started to tell her about cremation, a look of absolute horror crossed her face.

"You mean they are going to burn Nonna?"

I was so overcome, I could not reply. I realised that a child had put her finger on what is, in reality, an utterly barbaric thing to do, something beyond comprehension. How could I lamely explain that cremation was introduced as far back as the Stone Age and had been practised ever since? One day, when she is older, I shall have to ask Léa whether she remembers what I finally said.

As the months passed, however, the two of them began to talk about her in a most natural way, incorporating her into their conversations together. One day Léa said she wanted to write something about Nonna on my laptop. I was curious to see what she would say. It was this:

"I always laughed with my grandmother and she always laughed with me. My grandmother's name was Jean and she was the kindest woman ever. I loved her so much."

Léa's younger brother was not to be denied his turn:

"Every Christmas I whent in my grandfather's boat, one time my cousin's hat blow off her head. My time's with Jean were fun and cheerfull … I liked to have an icecream with my grandmother."

On 11 November of the year in which their Nonna died, I mentioned that it would have been her birthday. They took it up at once.

"Let's give Nonna a birthday party. Let's bake her a cake."

So we did. It was a splendid little family party and we all sang "Happy birthday, dear Nonna".

Had the shock of the cremation simply melted away into their psyches or did it linger, along with the other harsh lessons of life that beset a child's development?

The school years have brought added dimensions to my relationships with my grandchildren. Without any question, the initial struggle to learn to read and then the exquisite and growing delight at being able to do so have been defining features in their growth. Grandchild Four was so anxious to know what his elder sister was reading that, to the astonishment of his parents, he taught himself to read before he had started in Grade 0 at school. Small wonder then that his Grade 2 teacher was to award him a certificate of merit for "his outstanding reading and his unequalled, insatiable love of books and learning". As their expertise has flowered, all four successively have soaked themselves in the adventures of Harry Potter and multiple other stories.

As part of the tutoring of two of them while we were in the US, I read them the first half of George Orwell's *Animal Farm*. In no time, they knew the names of each and every animal on the farm and developed a chant based on the Seven Commandments developed by Snowball (good pig) and Napoleon (bad pig) and culminating in the triumphant line: "All animals are equal." I decided they were still too young to be taught the sequel: "All animals are equal but some are more equal than others." That would have to come as the realities of life and learning multiplied.

This once reluctant grandfather watches it all and realises what a rare, encompassing experience it is. Happiness, sadness; laughter, tears; love, hate: growing up.

Observations on
Mortality

That tree,
Olea africana: can it be
That it will outlive me?
That when I am ashes and dust
It will bend and thrust
In the gentle breezes of the night
And reach upwards to the morning light?

I am strong for now,
I roam, I run,
I write, I question how,
I respond to the rising and the setting of the sun.

Why then should I, the living mind
Housed in a robust frame,
Find myself consigned
To the dark from where I came
While the tree
Lives on,
Wild and free,
Long after I have gone?

Oh, *Olea*, I envy you
Your years of life to be.
On your leaves the morning dew,
In and on you, alive and free,
Birds of the vlei sing their song.
Is it wrong
To hope that, where I'll be,
When I call, they'll answer me?

Reflections

IT SEEMS TO ME APPROPRIATE that this essay, the penultimate in the collection, should be more reflective than those that have preceded it. I do not intend in the Orwellian sense to shoot any elephants although I may shoot down some myths and misconceptions.

As I have grown older, I have become increasingly conscious of the ordeal that my twin brother and I – both well and healthy in our eighties – caused my mother to go through in giving birth to the pair of us. She was slight in build and the stress of our birth, and its consequences, were to remain factors in her life for many decades. What I know of the circumstances leading up to our birth was recorded by my father in *Tales of*

Another Grandfather, which he wrote in old age for my two children and my brother's three. It has often proved to be a vital, and the only existing, link between his generation and those going back to his antecedents three generations back. This is what he recorded:

"When it became evident that Lucy was pregnant, we consulted my friend from DHS (Durban High School) schooldays, Dr Neil Campbell, who had just started up in private practice. He was very good to us, for Lucy was not having an easy pregnancy. After some months he told me that he suspected twins, but Lucy was not to know as it might upset her further.

"He decided to consult a specialist gynaecologist and, between them, they agreed that Lucy was too small and the babies too big to allow the normal nine months' period to run its course.

"So my poor darling was put into Rhodes Nursing Home and they 'induced labour' three weeks before the normal period. Lucy was in labour for five days and nights and had a hell of a time. Early on the morning of 3 April 1934 our first son was born. His name we had already decided was to be Jolyon. Half an hour later the Sister said to me, smoking endless cigarettes since about 5.30 a.m.: 'You have another son. What's his name?' With no chance to discuss the matter with my darling, who was 'out' by this time, I just said, drawing on *The Forsyte Saga* by John Galsworthy, which was much in vogue at the time as the source for both names, 'He's Michael.'

"I went up to the Nursing Home in the evening to find the 'nursery' packed with Durban doctors who had come to see 'Neil Campbell's twins'. 'They're not his twins,' I said indignantly, 'they're mine.'"

I have no evidence to prove it, and I never asked, although my brother confirms that this is correct, but my sense is that any question of further children from the marriage was ruled out, which, in turn, must have had consequences for their life together for decades to come.

However, my mother regained her health after our birth and lived an active life. But in our earlier years, and despite the help of a carer initially, she clearly bore the brunt of rearing not one but two lively babies. As other parents of twins will know, everything had to be done in duplicate, yet each child no doubt made its own individual demands on her. There can be no question that it must have been a hugely challenging time for someone who was new to marriage and motherhood. Each time I think of those days, I remind myself of how much my brother and I are indebted to her and yet, of course, at the time it was taken for granted that it was simply a mother's role, although in her case doubled up.

Our childhood was a secure and happy one and the compensation for my mother and father, if any was required within the circles in which they moved, was constant admiration of the "twins" of which, blissfully, we were unaware. I remember her, however, as the constant presence in our lives.

In maturer years, she returned to teaching and acted as headmistress for a period at the school where she taught. I recollect, though, that she suffered from a calcium deficiency that required bolstering, a direct result of what we took from her body. I have no doubt that my brother and I placed her physical condition under severe strain as we drew from her the lifeblood that has given us long and healthy lives.

She outlived my father, who died just short of his eightieth birthday. I shall never forget her death. At the age of eighty-three, she was living at Villa Assumpta, an old age home run by a Catholic order in the suburb of Wembley, high above the city of Pietermaritzburg. My brother, then Anglican Bishop of Natal, and his wife Dorrie, who were based in the city, used to visit her regularly, but I was living in Cape Town and saw her infrequently. When I did so, I found her frail and somewhat disoriented.

There came the day when my brother telephoned to say that she had had a relapse and was fading fast. I caught a late flight to Durban and hired a car to get to her. It was 10 p.m. when I arrived. My mother was unconscious and her breathing was staccato. I crouched by her bed and held her hand and told her I had come to be with her. As I spoke, there was the faintest squeeze of my hand. She had waited for me to arrive. She knew I was there. I continued to talk to her as time passed. On the stroke of midnight, the City Hall clock began to chime twelve times and the sound floated into her room. She was still alive when the chimes began and, when they ended, she had gone.

~

Having a twin brother was useful. There was always someone to build a chicken run with or hit a tennis ball to on the other side of the net or go looking for birds' eggs with or have an argument with or to have as company when it was time to go to sleep. Without knowing it, we bonded. My father notes in his *Tales of Another Grandfather* that, when we were very young, we hardly ever said "I". We always said "we". Among his teaching staff, he was known – "with a touch of malice, perhaps" – as "Our Father".

But we were different in nature and appearance. Michael always had a serious demeanour, a more disciplined approach to life. Without demur, he was first up in the morning to practise on the piano or feed the pigeons. There is a photograph of him (which now hangs behind his study door as a reminder of "a character feature which has persisted", as he puts it) weeding in our parents' garden at the age of six and another of me rollicking alongside him in a basket. I was a flibbertigibbet with a knack of shirking responsibility. Life was a jol. I got away with it to begin with, but it caught up with me in my teenage years.

Those years are difficult enough as it is but, in my case, they were compounded by constant comparisons between my twin brother and myself. It caused me to become something of a rebel. Michael did the right things, in the nicest possible way, without ever becoming even close to being a prig. He worked hard in class, his behaviour was immaculate, he mixed well with other boarders and he progressed steadily towards playing for Maritzburg College's celebrated first rugby XV in his matric year. Perhaps he had so-called teenage problems but I don't remember there being any.

It wasn't a case of envy. For one thing, he wore glasses, the prospect of which I abhorred. In truth, however, my eyesight had been affected after a bout of German measles when everything was still going well for me. One was supposed not to be exposed to direct sunlight during that time, but it happened a few days before I was due to play at scrumhalf in an Under-15 match between

Durban and Pietermaritzburg as a curtain-raiser to a Test match between the Springboks and the All Blacks. I told no one — and scored a try in front of thousands of spectators, including my father and Michael. But I bore the consequences: I became short-sighted.

In addition, as we entered our second-to-last year at school, I decided — as part of becoming a rebel, no doubt — to join the pranksters at the back of the class. An outcome of this was that, when the maths master asked me what the corresponding angle was of some diagrams he had drawn and numbered on the blackboard, I could not read what those numbers were. Although I knew the answer, I said I didn't know, all in the name of vanity. He threw the blackboard duster at me and told me I was going to fail maths in matric.

It was that sort of juvenile behaviour that caused the twins to be compared one with the other and drove us apart. Michael joined the fraternity of school prefects in our final year and proved the ideal candidate to head the House where "new boys" were accommodated, many of them boarders for the first time and suffering the pangs of homesickness.

It was a testing time for me but I pulled myself together in that matric year, sitting in the front row (where I did not need glasses!) and, taught by the headmaster himself, passed maths with ease and, with a distinction in English, achieved marginally better results than my brother.

The best possible thing that happened thereafter was that we went to separate universities, Michael living at home and attending the Pietermaritzburg campus of the University of Natal and I to the University of Cape Town where I flourished. I came home only twice a year, in July and at the year end. We went on family holidays either to the coast or inland where the trout streams were, and we got along fine.

While still working on his Honours degree in history at the University of Natal, Michael won a prestigious three-year scholarship to Cambridge (where he completed the degree before starting on a Master's) while I continued as a journalist in Durban with a Bachelor of Arts degree behind me. Out of the blue, he invited me at the end of his first year in Cambridge to join him for a tour to Rome and back on motorcycles. I jumped at the chance. When my company declined to second me to its London office for a period, telling me to be patient, I resigned and sailed for the UK. When I got there, I paid a courtesy call on the London editor and found there had been forces at work while I was en route. He offered me a permanent position on the staff. With that under my belt, I bought a BSA Bantam, as Michael had done, and we set off on our grand tour. It was a memorable time, full of adventures and stimulation, and we bonded in the old way. It has remained so ever since.

✢✣✤

An extraordinary coincidence was to occur in 1976. On New Year's Day, my twin became the Anglican Bishop of Pretoria and I went solo for the first time as manager of *The Pretoria News*. He and his family came from Grahamstown, where he had been Dean at the Cathedral, and I and my family from Johannesburg, where I had been senior assistant manager of *The Star*. For four years, before I moved on to head up my company's newspapers in Durban, the two families lived in the same city and saw each other frequently. He and I both had demanding jobs, his more so than mine because of the newness of the job, the vastness of his diocese and the range of commitments he had to undertake. But we took assurance from the support each was to offer the other.

In 2013, when my wife Jean died, Michael was instantly at my side. I flew at once to join him when his wife Dorrie died two months ago from the date I am writing this. "Neil Campbell's twins" have come a long way together. It has been an endearing journey.

Living Alone

I HAVE BEEN THROUGH VARIOUS traumas in my life — some of which seemed momentous at the time but less so in retrospect, and others which have stuck with me and play out from time to time in painful recollection. Childhood incidents tend to fall into the first category and those from adult life into the second. Taken collectively, they would probably be described by psychoanalysts as "character-building" on the basis that experiencing such traumas contributes to the rounding of a "whole" person.

Being enrolled at boarding school at the age of eight, which severed the umbilical cord with my parents for the first time, and then, three weeks later, being committed to an isolation ward at the school for ten days with measles, followed on the day of my release by being returned there for a further spell with chickenpox, was undoubtedly traumatic at the time. But the pain I experienced receded long ago and has come back to mind only because I dug deep into memory to locate such an example.

Being dropped as the first team scrumhalf early in the season in my final year at Maritzburg College while my twin brother continued as hooker – thus ending a partnership which went back to our Under-14 days – was extremely painful and humiliating, but it too faded in my memory. Or I thought it had until I picked up recently a history of College rugby teams and there, when it came to 1951, was the bald statement: "There was a weakness at scrumhalf which resulted in a replacement."

Did these traumas serve to form my character? In the sense that they taught me to live with setbacks, I suppose they did.

There have been others among what has been a fundamentally stimulating and fortunate life, but the most prolonged has been the experience of learning to live alone after forty-nine years of a happy marriage came to an abrupt end when my wife Jean died of a sudden illness. I experienced grief – raw, searing grief – for the first time.

It attacked me at unexpected moments

while, all the time, I was having to attend to the multiple requirements that go with the ending of someone's life. The person is no longer there in body, but her pillows are still there on the bed, her bath towel is on the rack and her toothbrush shares the same marble container as mine. Her scent emanates from her clothes in the walk-in dressing-room we shared.

The *Oxford Concise Dictionary* defines grief as "deep or violent sorrow". You cannot learn it until it happens to you personally.

I do not remember how long such intense grief lasted in my case, for the days and weeks and months seem, in recollection, to have passed in a haze. But at some stage it transmuted into the less acute sensation of mourning, a feeling of sadness, of emptiness (*Oxford Concise Dictionary*: "feel sorrow or regret, show conventional signs of grief for a period after a person's death"). A friend who had lost his wife many years before wrote to me: "Feel sad but try not to feel sorry for yourself. Remember the riches of your life together." I found it a useful reminder but easier said than done.

There developed the unexpected issue of how to fill my time. My days suddenly had lost their structure. It was as though I was having to start from scratch again to build a life. What helped was my decision to write about our years together after I found a set of cards and letters, wrapped in a red ribbon and labelled "From my husband", in a cardboard container. I meshed them together with the cards and letters I had received over the years and kept in a more random way, and found a narrative emerging.

I also decided to keep moving. I travelled a good deal, three times for lengthy spells in three years with my daughter and her family to the US where she and her husband had teaching assignments, four visits to family and friends in the UK with stimulating days in London, and trips to the Lake District to follow the trail of Wordsworth and to the Cotswolds and once to Italy to re-engage with old haunts. And I moved about in South Africa. I went to my cottage in Greyton every second weekend, but I could not bear to be there alone for more than one night. I invested more time in seeing old friends and making new ones.

But inevitably there were times on my own at home in Kommetjie. I was not good at it. The most painful moment of each day was turning the light out and trying to fall asleep alone in a double-bed. It seemed to me that, in my case, being on my own was not a natural condition.

I questioned others who lived alone to see if they could give me any guidance in how to set about it. Some of them, so used to it perhaps, seemed startled by the question. Others talked about becoming more involved in the community, joining organisations that worked among the poor, taking classes in subjects that might interest me. One person said I clearly needed therapeutic counselling. No one touched on an ache I felt within myself, and that was the sudden absence of the human warmth that had filled a greater part of my life. Once, after too many glasses of wine, I made a clumsy attempt to embrace one of those I was consulting about living alone, just to feel someone's arms around me, and received an instant rebuff.

As the months turned into years since I had become a widower — such a ghastly term — the more inquisitive among those I interacted with began to ask if I had met anyone who, y'know, I might want to, well — eh — marry. The answer was easy: no. I went out on a few dates, which were fun, but it was not something I could imagine and certainly not something I went in search of. One of the simple tests was: what would the reaction of my daughter or my son be to So-and-so? It always proved the clincher.

So I lived with loneliness as one, but only one, of the factors in my life. There were other factors that enriched me and stimulated me and helped to counter it. I expected it to be a constant in my life.

But recently, after years of this mix, something has happened. I have begun to become independent. I have started to move about in my own space without an empty feeling. I can go a whole day on my own, conversing only with a shop assistant, perhaps, or the petrol attendant I have become friendly with, and not feel lonely. I put out the bedside light at night and turn to sleep with thoughts in my head about what I will do tomorrow. Time to myself has become more precious. I don't mind being on my own. Writing these essays has helped enormously to reintegrate myself into my life as a whole from childhood through adulthood towards old age. It is an unexpected evolution and fills me at times with a headiness that is light-hearted. I want to dance and skip. I have regained a "something" that I thought I had lost forever.

Afterword:
Vintage Love

THE LOCAL TRAIN FROM Birmingham in the UK Midlands pulls up at a tiny station called Chester Road. There are only two people on the platform. I leave the train with my heart beating. Is one of them her?

As I approach, I realise it is not. Her younger sister — only just recognisable from sixty-six years ago — has come to meet me with her daughter. D—— no longer drives, they tell me — and is waiting at home.

My initial reluctance to make this visit turns to terror. If D—— has changed as much as her sister, the vision of her cool beauty I have carried all these years will be destroyed. The image of the girl who kissed me after the New Year's Eve dance as we sat in the back seat of that Buick, stuck to its gunnels in mud, will vanish. How very foolish to have put that at risk.

As I enter the lounge of her home, she is rising to her feet. I stare at her, astonished. Moments later, we fall into a warm embrace. It's the D— I remember: her teenage loveliness has matured into a timeless beauty. I cannot believe how deliriously happy I suddenly feel.

We sit together a little awkwardly on the couch while her family rustles about with preparations for tea. It dawns on me that we know so little of what the other has been doing since we last met. All I have learned is that her husband died five months ago after their lengthy marriage, her first, his second. On her side, she is aware that my wife died four years ago.

We begin to explore.

"How many children do you have?"

"Two. And you?"

"Three," she says, "and there are two from Alan's first marriage."

I cannot take my eyes off her. It is only later that she tells me that she too was terrified about our meeting again.

"It was only because my family had gone to such trouble that I felt I must go along with it. I need not have worried. I enjoyed it so much, though I found it all very emotional and am still feeling as though I am in another world. I shall remember it with pleasure but also with sadness that it was a one-off."

We graduate through tea and the late afternoon, learning more about each other, trying to fill in the gaps. "Do you remember …?" and "What happened to …?" punctuate our conservation. I feel reluctant to leave her when one of her sons is deputed to take me to the hotel where I am booked, to drop my bags. He says he will pick me up at 7 p.m.

I walk the grounds in a daze, trying desperately to accommodate my feelings. How can it be possible for my teenage infatuation with her — that calf love — to re-emerge in vintage form almost instantly upon seeing her again? Has it been preserved in aspic, only to be released so quickly? Or am I deceiving myself?

Sparkling wine is served before a handsome dinner and I engage in banter with her sons. What can they make of this elderly bloke from South Africa?

After dinner, the albums are brought out. I sense D——'s rising nostalgia as we look at browning photographs of our joint family holidays at that well-remembered farm. A feeling of tranquillity settles on me in place of the seething emotions of our opening encounter.

᠁

She comes to tea at my hotel next morning before I am to be dropped at the coach station for my onward journey to Oxford. She is wearing a crisp, long-sleeved shirt and sits close but erect on the couch with me. We have only one more hour together and we engage lightly in conversation although I feel an inner tension in us both. She smiles often, but she does not laugh, her beauty still contained. I hold her hand as we walk to the car that is to take me away. A farewell embrace, a quick wave from the car, and I return to another world.

On my last evening in England, I write:

"While having supper in a Cotswold restaurant two days after I left you, I tried to work out the best way of preventing my visit from being just a one-off. After ditching various heady options, I concluded that, if you agree, we should have for starters an email exchange in which we tell each other more about our lives, what has been happy and what has been sad."

And that is what we have done.

She tells me she did try to remain cheerful "while you were here with me but I am still in a state of misery a lot of the time since Alan died. I find Sundays difficult. Apart from the dear people who will ask me how I am, singing hymns is very hard. Alan loved singing and I find it hard not to cry, remembering his voice beside me." I recount to her how I learned to distinguish between grieving and mourning in the period after my wife died, and I stress to her that she is still very much in a state of grieving (experiencing deep, sometimes passionate sorrow and a strong sense of physical loss) and that, as time passes, this will become more a condition of mourning (to show grief for a period after a loved one's death). I warn her, however, that intense grief can recur, particularly on anniversaries and at traditional family gatherings, Christmas for example. She finds that so reassuring that she discusses it with her sons and her sister.

On one occasion, she writes:

"It is a pity we are so far away from each other. It would be lovely if we could get together more often."

In another exchange, I remind her about that New Year's Eve dance and the journey back in the mud.

"It was you who kissed me, you know. Not the other way round."

She will not be persuaded.

"I remember going to the dance, but I do not remember the drive back although my sister does. Have I repressed it?"

"You have definitely repressed it. Try to dig

deeper into your memory box. It was a beautiful experience for me and I would like to remember it with you."

A little later:

"It is good when one feels that one has helped others by spending time with them, by phone or email. I hope you can find the time to keep on doing it for me."

And my response:

"Whatever I can do now to be there for you in this difficult period of your life is an absolute pleasure. I want you to know that."

Then again: "This is two nights in a row that I have ended the evening writing to you. Thank you for being there for me to let off steam."

She tells me in a further message that two of her three sons have been to see her and are "slightly disapproving" of her correspondence with me. To my relief, a few days later she writes:

"By the way, don't think too much of my children's disapproval. They just seemed a bit cool about it and I realise now that I was probably expecting them to be as excited as I was about your visit and all the memories it evoked. I can write to whom I want, but I shall be more discreet in future."

During a visit to Natal, I drive up to the foothills of the Drakensberg to stay with a friend and on the way I pass the little hamlet of Boston.

There is the Farmers' Hall where the New Year's Eve dance took place — and probably still does. I find myself wondering how many hearts have been opened, and how many have been broken over the years.

I write to her:

"If you had been with me, perhaps it would have jolted your memory. Have you un-repressed your recollections by any chance?"

At last she budges. At the tail end of a lengthy message about various happenings in her life, she writes:

"I do remember going to the dance at Boston but I still think you made up the rest. On the other hand, I know I was a bit of a flirt in those days, so perhaps it is true. Happy memories either way."

By now, our relationship has reached the stage where it compares to a steady flame. I feel secure in it. Perhaps I shall travel to England to see her again. As she says, "It would be lovely ..." I would love her to visit me in Cape Town, but I suspect that would be asking too much. No matter. Our bond has become like a mature wine from a particularly fine vintage.

About the Author

As AN EARLY TINKERER WITH words, Jolyon Nuttall chose a career in journalism, working in London and New York during a nine-year stint attached to *The Daily News* in Durban. His move to the ranks of management held the wordsmith at bay. He rose to become General Manager of *The Star* and a director of Argus Newspapers Ltd. during the hectic 1980s. Since being freed of those preoccupations, his writing instincts have resurfaced. He has self-published works on his father's lifelong relationship with Alan Paton, entitled *A Literary Friendship*, and on flyfishing, in a book of essays entitled *Hooked on Rivers*, which sold out after two editions. He lives on the edge of the sea in Kommetjie, near Cape Point, where he is at peace to write. A further work is all but complete.